Pathway to
PURPOSE

Deborah Joyner Johnson

Pathway to
PURPOSE

Deborah Joyner Johnson

MorningStar Publications
A DIVISION OF MORNINGSTAR FELLOWSHIP CHURCH
P.O. Box 440
Wilkesboro, NC 28697

Pathway to Purpose
Deborah Joyner Johnson
Copyright © 2005

International Standard Book Number—1-929371-53-5

Cover Design: Nicole Beals/Inside Layout: Sharon Whitby

All Scriptures are New International Version unless otherwise indicated.

DEDICATION

This book is lovingly dedicated to my children:
Matthew, Meredith, and Abby,
who have given my life inspiration and joy.

May you faithfully pursue and finish
all that you have been called to do.

♦ ♦ ♦ ♦ ♦

To my brother, Rick:

I am sincerely grateful for your help with this book.

Thank you for encouraging me and multitudes
of others to push forward to fulfill our callings.

May you wholeheartedly and successfully
complete your course.

♦ ♦ ♦ ♦ ♦

To my dear friend, Deb Williams:

My sincerest and heartfelt appreciation for
your many hours of assistance with this book.

I will always treasure our friendship.

♦ ♦ ♦ ♦ ♦

To Steve Thompson:

Thank you for reading this manuscript
and for giving me guidance and ideas
about how to move forward.

You are an inspiration to many.

♦ ♦ ♦ ♦ ♦

TABLE OF CONTENTS

FOREWORD

There is an exciting calling and purpose on the life of every believer. II Timothy 1:9 says God **"has saved us and called us with a holy calling, not according to our works, but according to His own purpose and grace which was granted us in Christ Jesus from all eternity."**

He has prepared and designed a purpose for you that is uniquely individual. Most Christians believe this, but never fully enter into their potential in the Lord because they are not willing to pay the necessary price to truly fulfill it, just as Jesus lamented: **"for many are called, but few are chosen" (Matthew 22:14).**

That realization led my sister, Debbie, to write *Pathway to Purpose.* In this timely and important book, she examines the lives of six inspiring individuals who accomplished the extraordinary. By following the lives of these remarkable people and learning the lessons that their stories teach, you will find that you, too, can press beyond the limits and experience the fullness of all that God has purposed for you.

Our times require a breed of Christians who will never be content with mediocrity, but rather choose to push beyond the average and live their lives on a level few ever know. As you read this book, be prepared to be challenged into greatness as you carve your own path to fulfill your purpose.

Rick Joyner

INTRODUCTION

A life filled with purpose has power. Those who have this power will often accomplish great things. This book is about six extraordinary people, from different backgrounds and professions, who were all successful in achieving remarkable goals in their lives. They were able to learn from their mistakes, rather than being stopped by them. Other obstacles motivated them, inspiring them to work even harder to finish what they had started. They not only saw their own goals accomplished, but they also left a legacy behind that benefited many others.

Those who accomplish great things not only have vision, but also an intense passion for their work. Passion fuels their focus, devotion, and perseverance. Passion is also what separates the dreamers who want to accomplish great things but never seem able to get their visions off the ground, from those who see their dreams fulfilled. The point of this study is to understand how to add these essential ingredients to a vision so it can be realized.

As we study what it takes to accomplish something of significance, we will also address some problems that can stop us from fulfilling a life of purpose—fear, procrastination, impatience, discouragement, or guilt from the past. As we examine these problems, we will also discuss how to not only recognize when they are making inroads into our lives, but how to overcome them.

There is a satisfaction in accomplishing anything of significance, but there is something even more fulfilling than that. We were each created with a purpose. As the Scriptures testify, we were known by the Lord from the foundation of the world—He foresaw each of our lives and gave us our purpose in them. Not only is there a great sense of life and vision which increases in the discovery of our own unique purpose, but we will also have a greater fellowship with the Lord. The most wonderful part about accomplishing what we have been born to do is knowing that we are doing His will. Our individual purpose in life is bigger than us, which links us together in fellowship with the King and His people—the truest reward of all.

C.S. Lewis once said: "You are never too old to set another goal or to dream a new dream." It is possible to overcome any failures and hindrances that have stopped you in the past. My prayer is that the fire which was ignited in the lives of these extraordinary people will light your life with power in your purpose, enabling you to accomplish everything that you have been born to do.

Deborah Joyner Johnson

CHAPTER ONE

THE POWER OF VISION

MARTHA BERRY, A TRUE VISIONARY

"I have walked too far on my
plank of faith to turn back."
~Martha Berry

Jonathan Swift once said: "Vision is the art of seeing the invisible." Martha Berry had this type of vision. At a time when women were seldom educated beyond finishing school, and even public schools were rare, her vision was to begin a school for impoverished boys in the mountains of Georgia. Through the power of vision, perseverance, and courage she established one of the nation's most successful work-study schools.

As the times changed, her vision increased and she was able to use these changes as opportunities for even further advancement. Through the years, that one little school eventually expanded to become Berry College, which is now the number two undergraduate comprehensive college in the South, as stated by *U.S. News & World Report, 2005.*

From a one-room school to a remarkable college— what a legacy! However, few such accomplishments are made without obstacles, adversity, and even tragedy, and Martha had her share of these. Even so, she also had the resolve not to let anything keep her from finishing what she felt called to do. May the power of her vision light your own. This is her story.

MARTHA'S FOUNDATION

Martha was born in Rome, Georgia on October 7, 1866. This was right after the Civil War had ended and the South, especially Georgia, still lay devastated. She was the second of eight children born to Captain and Mrs. Thomas Berry. Her family had wealth and social prestige, yet this did not compel Martha to seek that same kind of lifestyle for herself.

Four people had significant and positive influences in Martha's life, from which her unique character was built. The first was a former slave she called "Aunt Martha." She was the overseer of the kitchen and helped supervise the children. Aunt Martha had a strong religious faith, and from her, young Martha learned that there was a Scripture for every situation in life.

Ida McCullough was the second. She was the governess for the Berry children, who would often take Martha on walks in the woods teaching her about nature. She learned through Miss Ida to observe, listen, and appreciate the beauty of nature through God's eyes.

The third was Frances Berry, Martha's mother, who was caring, frugal, and kind. She managed the family's money and time like she was running a business. The skills Martha learned from her mother would later pay great dividends in her own life's purpose.

Last was Captain Berry, her father, who had the most positive influence in Martha's life. Since he was so important to her accomplishments, a brief summary of his life will help us understand how he affected Martha so greatly.

As a young man, Thomas Berry began his career in Rome, Georgia as an apprentice to a storekeeper. He was quickly promoted to partner and later opened a store of his own. He soon opened a cotton brokerage, which became very successful because of his astute business skills.

War was imminent with Mexico, so soon Berry had to leave his family and business to serve in the Mexican War from 1846-48, where he earned the rank of captain for his bravery. When he returned home, he worked diligently and his business continued to flourish. He then bought Oak Hill plantation, where Martha later grew up with every available luxury. All was well until the Civil War began.

Captain Berry had to leave his family, home, and business again to serve in the Confederate army. When the war finally ended, he returned home and thankfully found his family well and Oak Hill still standing. However, his fields were burned, and there were no fences or cattle. All of his hard-earned Confederate money was now worthless, which left no money to buy the much needed seed to replant his cotton. Still, Captain Berry did not let these problems stop him from continuing on with his dream of rebuilding the cotton brokerage and the land that was flourishing before the war.

There was no other place to secure a loan but from the very ones against whom he had just been fighting in the Civil War. Yet Captain Berry held no bitterness. Humbly, he went to Philadelphia and spoke to a group of Yankee financiers about how they all had the common goal of restoring the Federal Union of the States. They had trusted him before the war and he asked them to trust him again by giving him a loan to rebuild his business. Because of his humility and courage, he received a standing ovation and they loaned him $50,000. With this money Captain Berry rebuilt his business, repaid the loan, and soon became even more prosperous than he had been before the war.

Captain Berry was a man of his word, generous, diligent, a leader in the community, a friend to many, and had a strong religious faith. Martha would also grow to characterize these attributes which defined her father's success.

He often took Martha, even at a very young age, to visit the poor whose farms had been ruined; he never sheltered her from the destruction that the war had caused. Because of this, she developed an interest in the less fortunate children in the surrounding area. Martha and her father frequently gave food, clothing, and money to these destitute families in the hills of Georgia. He taught her that "giving was not a duty; it was the natural way to live." Consequently, it was no surprise that many times by her own choice, Martha returned from their visits without her coat, shoes, or hair ribbons.

When Martha was sixteen, she was sent to a finishing school in Baltimore, which she disliked very much. She wrote home saying that she did not belong there and that the girls made fun of her clothes. Her father's reply by wire was this:

> A BERRY NEVER FORSAKES A GOAL UNTIL IT IS ATTAINED. DO NOT COME HOME. YOU WILL BE SENT BACK TO BALTIMORE ON NEXT TRAIN. PAPA

At the time, Martha felt the answer was cold and heartless. She did not know how much her father missed her, and that he had to set aside his feelings because her father "knew how necessary it was for Martha to finish what she had started." Through this, he taught her an important lesson about never giving up. He did, however, send money for her to buy the latest fashions and Martha soon began to fit in. Even so, she felt the reasons for her acceptance were really "snobbish and false." Martha realized the importance of not judging a person on the outside, but by what was on the inside.

Sadly, when Martha returned home at the end of the school term, she learned that her father had had a stroke. She spent as much time as possible with him, and during one of those visits he told her that he was leaving her eighty-three acres across the road from Oak Hill, and that the land would be income for her in the years to come. He also told Martha, "You have giving hands…I'm proud of that. A person knows very little about the art of living until he learns to give." Martha treasured those words and resolved to portray their meaning. Before long, Captain Berry had another stroke and died shortly thereafter. Although Martha was heartbroken, she knew all he had taught her would remain with her forever.

HER VISION BEGINS

When Martha was small, her parents had built their children a log cabin as a playhouse. As a teenager, she went there on many Sunday afternoons to play her melodeon and read. The turning point of her life began in this log cabin. While reading one Sunday afternoon in 1900, she saw three boys in ragged overalls peeping through the cabin door. She invited them in, gave them apples to eat, and told them Bible stories. Since she was a gifted storyteller, they listened intently, and she asked them to come again the next Sunday and bring someone with them. They did. Soon young and old alike came to listen to Martha tell her Bible stories. By autumn, the cabin was overflowing with people every Sunday afternoon.

Her brothers, sisters, and friends complained that all the traffic from wagons, mules, oxcarts, and people on foot were upsetting their Sundays. Being the considerate person that she was, Martha moved her Sunday classes seven miles from Oak Hill to an abandoned, dilapidated chapel in Possum Trot. There they had more room and would not bother anyone. With the help of the hill people, they refurbished the little chapel until it looked like new.

She encouraged them for all that they had accomplished, helping them feel that this chapel was their own. She taught Bible stories to pupils of all ages along with her sister, Frances, who became her assistant. Soon the mountain people became the focus of her life, and before long she became known as "The Sunday Lady."

Martha was beautiful and had a wonderful personality which not only attracted people, but made them feel special. Her sisters said she was the most popular one of them and had many suitors. But the desire to help her new friends became stronger than romantic interests. The words of her father rang in her ears, "These people don't want charity. They want help to help themselves. It's up to us to help them do that."

A DREAM COMES TRUE

With the help of the mountain people, they were able to restore three more chapels for her Sunday schools within a few years. However, she began to understand that the children needed more than Bible stories—they needed to learn how to read, write, and do arithmetic, as well as learn hygiene and ways to earn a living. Her vision was clear, her dream now birthed. Martha Berry knew her purpose in life was to educate the children in the impoverished, north Georgia mountains.

Against the advice of family and friends, she built a school on the property her father had given her. With one hundred dollars of her own money for lumber, a carpenter she hired, and the help of some of the larger boys to clear the land, her one-room schoolhouse was built. She loved plants, so she placed shrubs and flowers around the foundation. One of her well-known sayings was "One can't teach beauty; it must be lived." And another familiar saying was she loved growing "trees, flowers, and people." Her school characterized the essence of beauty.

Although she did not feel prepared to teach from her education from Miss Ida and the finishing school, she went forward with her vision. She opened the doors of the Boys Industrial School (BIS) as the lone teacher with only Frances to assist her. Still, Martha's school grew despite opposition from her family, irregular attendance of students, and the resistance of some parents. Soon, she added two wings and a steeple to the one-room building. But, she needed more help. She went to the county board and they agreed to hire two teachers, but only if Martha would contribute to their salaries and buy school supplies with her own money.

HER VISION EXPANDS

As the school continued to grow that first year, she added another teacher, Elizabeth Brewster, who had the same heart and philosophy in education as Martha. Elizabeth stayed with Martha for twenty years. Soon they had four day schools started in surrounding areas. But many children were still too far away from the schools, so bad weather kept them from coming. And when spring came, it was time for plowing. As a result, school attendance was irregular and they would slip into the old ways of home—not washing their hands, bringing frogs and snakes inside, and so on.

Martha found it difficult to train them under these circumstances. They needed consistency in their lives. Thus, her vision expanded to include a boarding school. As she visualized the whole innovative project, it would be a school where "boys could come and stay, the subjects would be related to their needs—agriculture as well as arithmetic, dairying as well as geography, marketing as well as grammar...a work-study program." If a boy could not pay tuition, room, and board, he would earn his way through school by working. "He would be surrounded by learning, cleanliness, and beauty. And when he finished his studies, he would be a practical example of 'Christian citizenship' wherever he went."

But to build a boarding school, the law required that she would have to transfer ownership of her land to the school. Judge Moses Wright, a friend, advised her against this even though he admired her courage and selfless caring for the mountain people. "Martha, once you give this property away, you can't get it back." Her reply was: "I understand...don't you see I want the poor boys and girls of the rural South to be my heirs?" She had a big heart and wanted to provide an education for children "who never had a chance."

Most people in the community doubted her dream, even most of her family. "Martha was not about to doubt her dreams just because others did. Besides, it was more than a dream now. It was a God-given purpose to which she was ready to devote her entire life. 'I'm going to step on a plank of faith,' she said. 'Let's get our first dormitory started!'"

And then, completely in character, Martha said, "My school is not going to have a makeshift look. The buildings and grounds must be designed for a beautiful effect as well as usefulness." So she hired an architect and arranged an account of $2,500 to cover expenses for the ten-room dormitory. After it was built, Martha said, "I think it is one of the most beautiful buildings in the world! We will honor our first real teacher by naming it Brewster Hall."

HANDS, HEAD, AND HEART

Her dormitory school opened on January 13, 1902, and by the end of the school year, eighteen boarding students were enrolled. Martha had the dream that education was the head, heart, and hands and it was taught this way, as exemplified in the work-study program.

Martha taught religion as a part of daily living. She had a very strong prayer life and truly believed that *prayer changes things*. She kept that motto on her desk where she could see it daily. "She and the Almighty were on good terms, and talking to her God was as natural an expression of her inner self as was laughter. To her, prayer was also listening." She enjoyed having conversations with God as she would talk to a friend.

She designed a school shield with four emblems that depicted her philosophy of education:

1) The Cabin—for Simplicity in Living
2) The Plow—for the Dignity of Labor
3) The Lamp—for Academic Excellence, and
4) The Bible—for Prayer and Christian Principles

EDUCATION AND WORK PROGRAM

Martha moved from her home at Oak Hill to the school so she could spend more time with the boys. The boys had to work two hours a day from the beginning. "Wood must be chopped, land cleared, fences built, stumps dug, clothes, floors, dishes washed, lamp wicks trimmed, lamp chimneys polished, the garden hoed— the job list seemed endless." Not only did she conduct a good education and work program, but she also spent evenings with her students popping corn and talking, which helped many of them get over missing their families so much.

Martha was always planning. One day the boys were placing a double row of elm trees from the road to an elevated area. Her friend, Judge Wright, was watching. "Martha, what do you mean, spoiling a perfectly good field with a string of shade trees?" She replied, "Why, Moses, these elms are to line a new road we want to build." Puzzled, he said, "Road? Road to where?" Martha simply replied, "To that knoll where the recitation hall will go up." In just a few years there was a recitation hall in that very spot and it looked just like Martha had envisioned. This is true vision—seeing the invisible become visible.

Next, she planned to build a barn because they had just been given a cow in answer to a prayer. But not just any barn—it would have a spire just like a church to remind the boys "that their work can be a part of worship every day." The first school year ended and ten boys stayed on that summer to build another log dormitory and a dairy. Elizabeth Brewster was thrilled. She wrote, "Our little country school was beginning to take on the appearance of an institution." By the beginning of the next school year in 1903, they had accommodations for sixty students.

TRAGEDY COMES

The second year was marked with tragedy when their beloved schoolhouse burned to the ground, even though many of the boys risked their lives trying to save it. Classes had to be held in the dormitory, and because of the fire, many financial needs accumulated. "Never before had she been forced to ask for money, but since the future of the Appalachian children was at stake, she swallowed her pride" and asked for money, just as her father had done so many years before.

She began a long campaign to raise funds for BIS. She traveled from Rome, Georgia to Atlanta, then to Washington D.C., and New York. While she was in New York, she looked up a man she knew donated to worthy causes, R. Fulton Cutting. He asked her, "What is your pay for all this work?" With her usual enthusiasm, she replied, "I get everything out of it, Mr. Cutting—all the thrill of watching these neglected, illiterate boys turn into clear-thinking, educated, young men who will return to their communities to change them!" When she told him it cost $50 a year to send a boy to her school, he took out his checkbook and gave her $500. That was the first of many donations to her school and the beginning of thousands of miles of travel through the years in fund-raising. Before long they rebuilt the schoolhouse and continued educating the underprivileged boys. Even through the Depression in 1907, her school survived.

Sometime later the governor of Georgia invited her to a reception and introduced her to Andrew Carnegie. She eagerly told him all about her boys. Later he gave her a promise of $50,000 if she could raise another $50,000. Amazingly, she did with his help. After the BIS had been operating for five years, the school had grown to six buildings and was situated on one thousand acres.

MARTHA MEETS THE PRESIDENT

Many others began to take notice of Martha Berry and her work with the mountain people. Even President Theodore Roosevelt wanted to meet her the next time she came to Washington, D.C. When she was able to visit the President, he said, "America needs more citizens like you, Miss Berry, who are not afraid to dream big and who know how to turn their dreams into practical accomplishments. And I like to see a woman do it, by jolly!" He told her that when he was finished being President, he was going to Rome, Georgia to take a look at her school. And he did. The cottage in which he dined became known as the Roosevelt cabin. A phrase from one of his speeches became a school slogan: "Be a lifter, not a leaner." Later Martha changed the slogan to a like meaning: "Not to be ministered unto; but to minister."

Theodore Roosevelt told her that she should start a school for girls, thus inspiring another huge dream. Martha worked on this full force and opened her school for girls on Thanksgiving Day, 1909. Many of the girls were admitted with working scholarships just like the boys. Of course, they had their own dormitory and were educated separately, as such were the times. The name of the school was changed from the Boys Industrial School to The Berry Schools. The girls' first graduating class was in 1914.

NOTHING BUT THE BEST

Each teacher at Berry taught a variety of subjects along with good behavior and courtesy. Martha wanted her teachers to be the very best instructors. "No one is going to do a thing better than we do it at Berry!" So, she sent a teacher named Willie Sue Cordell to the best studio at Berea College in Kentucky, which excelled in weaving and baking. After studying with the famous instructors, she taught what she learned to the girls at Berry. Willie Sue also developed an excellent crafts center at Berry.

The Berry Schools continued to grow with new students, buildings, and land being added. President

Woodrow Wilson, an educator himself, praised Martha's work. By the time World War I began, she saw five hundred of her boys and alumni (including some staff members) march off to war leaving the operation of the school to women and young boys. One captain of the war wrote Martha, "Our Company includes seven of your students. They can do anything—build a bridge, cook, make beds, conduct a funeral, or just be quiet and behave! I want you to know your training is the best!" Martha was so proud of her boys.

HENRY FORD

The war ended and expansion continued with The Berry Schools, which became accredited in 1923. In the early 1920s, Henry Ford became a close friend to Martha. Since he was a "self-made man," she thought if she invited him to her campus, he just might appreciate the work program at Berry. He did. He sent a business associate to study the needs of the school. Through Mr. and Mrs. Ford's generosity, they built a girls' dormitory, a modern kitchen and dining hall, and The Quadrangle, which eventually included an auditorium, weaving room, gift shop, library, gymnasium, second dormitory, and heating facilities. Mr. Ford insisted that the buildings be of the finest quality and built of limestone from a local quarry. Mr. Ford said, "I gave to her because I felt she could make better use of some of my money than I could myself."

BERRY COLLEGE

As a visionary, Martha embraced the changing world and rising educational standard. In 1926 she started

Berry College—a coeducational junior college. In 1930, it was expanded to a four-year college, and in 1972, graduate programs were added. Martha's theories were progressive. "All over the South, journals and newspapers began suggesting that farmers adopt Berry techniques." They experimented with the latest methods in crop rotation, forestry, farming, and agricultural sciences." Her boys had produced the "finest herd of dairy Jerseys in the entire South, and their breeding cattle were winning blue ribbons in three states." The reforestation program yielded amazing harvests by many farmers in surrounding areas. All of these projects produced money for Berry College.

Martha was so pleased with her students. When the twenty-fifth anniversary of her school came in 1927, she told her students, "I thank you for giving me a perfect silver 'wedding' anniversary...Love is the greatest thing in the world!" Even in 1929 when the American economy collapsed, her school stayed open, and the waiting list was the longest it had ever been. Martha believed that it was the hard times that brought the best out of people, making them stronger.

HOUSE OF DREAMS

She was so loved by her students that they built her a "House of Dreams," which still stands today. Emily Hammond also generously helped with finances in building Martha's home. Martha would show people her new home and proudly say, "The girls hooked these rugs and wove the curtains...and aren't the baskets lovely?" Baskets and flowers were everywhere in her home. Also, she frequently wore dresses made from the materials woven by the girls who worked in the handcraft shop. She seemed to always be encouraging the students for their fine work. Martha Berry was a favorite among the students and they chose to honor her on Mountain Day, which is celebrated in remembrance of her birthday of October 7.

In her late sixties, Martha's health began to deteriorate. She had a serious heart condition and high blood pressure. Though she was becoming more weary, Berry College was still very much on her heart. In 1940, when she was invited to Texas, along with 1,500 other guests and celebrities by the Variety Clubs of America, awarding her with the tribute of "The American who did more than any other for humanity this year," she determined she would go. Her doctor told her that a train trip to Texas would be terrible for her heart. He also warned her that it would be too exciting to speak in front of all those show people. Martha still went. During her acceptance speech she said: "My doctor told me I couldn't make a long train trip, but he didn't say I couldn't fly. He told me I couldn't make a speech, but he didn't say I couldn't talk…." The celebrities jumped to their feet, roaring with laughter and gave her a standing ovation. Everywhere she went, people admired Martha Berry for her contributions.

Martha's eyesight was failing and soon she was having to stay in bed because of her heart. But for as long as she could, she dictated letters on behalf of Berry College and answered as many questions as possible about the campus. She knew her time was coming near and that "the vision to which she had committed her life was more meaningful than ever." On February 27, 1942, at the age of seventy-five, Martha Berry passed away. In a letter attached to her will, Martha left these words: "When I am gone, I want you to always think of me as alive—alive beyond your furthest thoughts, and near and loving you, and growing more like God wants me to become."

Martha Berry's memory is still alive in her beloved Berry College. Her accomplishments were vast. From the original eighty-three acres, the campus is now 28,000 acres—one of the largest in the world. Thousands of students have graduated from Berry College, which now includes nearly forty structures, most of them built by students. Today, Berry College offers graduate and undergraduate programs. Since 1985, when *U.S. News & World Report* began publishing its rankings of the South's best colleges, Berry College has had high rankings and as mentioned is ranked second today. It is still a model for colleges in the United States and abroad, offering work experience as part of every student's development. It has a "Religion-in-Life Program" with an interdenominational Christian campus congregation. Today Berry College still encourages its students and graduates to be more and do more for others and themselves.

Martha was given eight honorary doctorates from outstanding universities. She also served on many boards in Georgia, was voted one of America's twelve outstanding women in *Good Housekeeping's* magazine contest, and is listed on Ida Tarbell's list of America's Fifty Greatest Women. She received numerous medals and was invited to court by Queen Mary as a "salute to education in America." Three Presidents visited her— including President Coolidge who presented her with the Roosevelt Memorial Association's Medal for Distinguished Service in 1925. "The citation was for 'the distinguished service...of one, who seeing a great need, turned from pleasant places in which her lines were cast to bring light and opportunity to children, who, but for her, would have walked all their lives in the shadow of ignorance.'" Her response was: "Mr. President, I accept this honor humbly for myself but proudly for my boys and girls." It was her love for her students that gave her the power and strength to accomplish her extensive vision.

CONCLUSION

As a child, Martha received an excellent foundation from the loving people who surrounded her. As a teenager, she modeled what she had learned. She grew into an adult with uncompromising character who birthed a vision and never let it die. With great personal sacrifice, she worked until her vast dreams came true. Her vision was clear on the path she followed, and love was the guide.

Martha did not know the meaning of impossible. She reached her goals with unyielding passion and faith believing that **"...all things are possible with God" (Mark 10:27).** Alice Wingo, a former Dean of Women at Berry College, once said this: "We never say to Miss Berry that something cannot be done. If she asks to have this dormitory moved over to the log cabin campus in the morning, we just answer, 'What time did you want it there, Miss Berry?'" With that kind of resolve and faith, all things are possible!

Once we can "see" what our purpose is in life, then we will have the necessary vision to accomplish it. We should never lose sight of the vision. If we do, our focus will become clouded, rendering us useless, and we will not finish what we have been called to do. We must keep Proverbs 29:18 in mind: **"Where there is no vision, the people perish..." (KJV).**

As we stay focused on our purpose, never giving up, believing in faith that we can fulfill it, we will then do it. God has given us the power to complete all that He has called us to do. Philippians 4:13 says: **"I can do all things through Him who strengthens me."** The Lord will give us strength to do what may seem impossible. By keeping our vision in focus, it will be accomplished.

May we learn from Martha Berry that with the power of vision, anything is possible for those who have the faith to follow and finish their course.

A vision without a task is but a dream.
A task without a vision is drudgery.
A vision and a task together are the hope of the world.
~ Found in a church in Essex, England, 1730.

Some information and all quotes for this chapter were taken from Martha Berry, A Woman of Courageous Spirit and Bold Dreams by Joyce Blackburn, Peachtree Publishers, 1992. Other information was provided by the Oak Hill Online Museum website: www.berry.edu/oakhill and Berry College website: www.berry.edu

CHAPTER TWO

THE POWER OF PASSION

THE LEGACY OF C.S. LEWIS

If you read history, you will find that the Christians
who did the most for the present world were just
those who thought the most of the next.
~ C.S. Lewis

Passion is the power that ignites our vision. C.S. Lewis had this type of passion in writing, and he is still one of the most popular Christian writers today.

Lewis began writing before he was a Christian. A few of his early works include Lewis' first anthology, *Spirits in Bondage* (1919), which was published under the pseudonym Clive Hamilton. He also wrote a highly acclaimed book-length narrative poem in 1926 entitled, *Dymer*, under that same name. But it was only after he became a Christian, and grew to be so passionate in his beliefs, that he began writing prolifically. As we take a glimpse at his life, we will soon understand how his journey to Christianity paved the way to his passionate writings. The following is his inspiring story.

HIS EARLY LIFE

Clive Staples Lewis was born on November 29, 1898 in Belfast, Ireland (now Northern Ireland). He was the second son to Albert and Flora Lewis. Clive, who liked to be called Jack, had a happy childhood. His parents were financially stable, cultured, and intellectual. He enjoyed playing with his brother, Warren while he was young, and as they grew older, they continued to remain very close.

Two imaginative people influenced Lewis in his early childhood—his father and his nurse. It is very possible that these two began the nurturing of his creative mind at an early age. Jack's father had a unique talent. "At times he was quite humorous, and his sons even claimed he was the best storyteller in the world as he always acted out the character parts."[1] Their nurse, Lizzie Endicott, was great fun; she would tell Jack and Warren of Irish folklore and legend. "How her two, small charges loved to snuggle up to her on cold, dark nights to hear stories of leprechauns and giants, of mythical beasts and gallant knights rescuing damsels in distress."[2]

Jack loved Beatrix Potter's books, and at age five he began writing very imaginative stories. "Because of Beatrix Potter, Clive naturally involved animals (in his writing) but, as he also loved Lizzie Endicott's accounts of medieval chivalry, he combined the two."[3] Little did he know then the extent that this gift of writing would develop later in his life.

"The family home, called 'Little Lea,' was a large, gabled house with dark, narrow passages and an overgrown garden, which Warnie (Warren) and Jack played in and explored together."[4] The new house was tremendous and the upper stories had useless rooms, attics, and many closets. Lewis had a grand time exploring the house. This may have been where some of his ideas were derived in his famous *Chronicles of Narnia* books.

Young Lewis enjoyed reading. "There was also a library that was crammed with books—two of Jack's favorites were *Treasure Island* by Robert Louis Stevenson and *The Secret Garden* by Frances Hodgson Burnett."[5] These two books are very imaginative, and the love of these types of books was birthed within him when he was just a child. Most writers tend to write similarly to what they love to read, for that is where their passion is ignited. C.S. Lewis was no different.

All was well with Lewis until his mother died of cancer in 1908. Lewis missed her terribly, and to make matters worse, just a little over a month after she died, their father sent the boys to a boarding school named Wynyard in England. They hated Wynyard because it seemed more like a prison camp than school. Lewis missed Belfast terribly and when the school closed in 1910, he happily returned home.

The following year he was sent to nearby Campbell College in Belfast, which he thoroughly enjoyed. It was at Campbell that he first began to appreciate poetry. He read a poem by Matthew Arnold and the details were so graphic that it seemed he could see and touch everything. "...A yearning engulfed him. He felt like an explorer aspiring to reach some far-off goal yet not knowing in which direction to go."[6]

Lewis did not complete his first term at Campbell due to a terrible cough. He was sent home to recuperate, and he enjoyed the time with his father. After the holidays, though, he began attending Cherbourg Preparatory School, which he liked (Cherbourg was part of Malvern College where he would later finish school). A teacher named Miss Cowie was a favorite with Lewis as she reminded him of his nurse. Sadly though, she exposed him to different religious faiths which challenged his belief in God. Lewis had been raised Protestant, and after the death of his mother, he began reading the Bible, working out his own ideas on religion. This helped to console him when he was sad or lonely. But with Miss Cowie's influence, Jack, then a young teenager, began reading material on every type of faith. Mythology became one of his chief interests. Consequently, he gave up his Christian faith and became an atheist.

In 1916, Lewis continued to enjoy reading creative books such as George McDonald's *Phantastes*. Reading this book seemed to open the door even further to his growing imagination.

C.S. LEWIS AS A YOUNG MAN

In 1917, Lewis began attending the University College in Oxford. However, within a few months he volunteered for active duty with the British Army in World War I. He was wounded in the Battle of Arras on April 15, 1918, but after six months of recovery, he returned to battle. During the war, he made friends with Paddy Moore. They made a promise to each other that if either of them died,

Lewis would take care of Paddy's mother, or Paddy would take care of Lewis' father. Paddy died in the war, and Lewis dutifully fulfilled his promise by taking care of Paddy's mother for thirty years until she died. Beyond the promise, he also supported Maureen, Paddy's younger sister. Admirably, Lewis was a man of his word.

Thankfully, the war ended in 1918 and Lewis was discharged in December 1919. "Lewis returned to Oxford, where he took up his studies again with great enthusiasm. In 1925, after graduating with first-class honors in Greek and Latin Literature, Philosophy and Ancient History, and English Literature, Lewis was elected to an important teaching post in English at Magdalene College, Oxford. He remained at Oxford for twenty-nine years."[7] He later began teaching Medieval and Renaissance English at Cambridge until the summer of 1963. In all this he was well-respected in his field.

Being an atheist at the time, Lewis tried to stay away from those who called themselves Christians. Several of his closest friends who were not Christians began "questioning the source of life and the universe and Jack became thoroughly disillusioned. When they finally defected to Christianity, he was deeply offended…"[8] Soon after, he met a very intelligent man named Neville Coghill. Lewis enjoyed talking about the books they read, their studies, and even Christianity. "Jack scoffed at those fools who rely on religion for moral support. To Jack's amazement, instead of eagerly agreeing with him, his companion unashamedly announced that he was a Christian!"[9] Lewis just could not understand. He soon discovered that even some of his favorite authors were Christians—Milton, George Herbert, John Donne, Spencer, and MacDonald. He could not seem to escape Christians.

A CHANGED MAN

Surprisingly, Lewis became friends with J.R.R. Tolkien at Magdalene College; "Not only was he a dedicated Christian, he was one of the worst kind—a Roman Catholic, with whom Jack had vowed *never* to associate."[10] In 1929, Lewis' father died, and he felt an extreme loss. Lewis felt backed into a corner and he knew then that he only had one place to turn.

Consequently, in 1929, he began reading Christian books again, contemplating everything he read. One evening J.R.R. Tolkien and other friends challenged Lewis to seriously think about Jesus. As he was trying to sleep one evening, he wrestled with the concept of Jesus as God in the flesh. Almost two weeks later he wrote Tolkien, "I have passed on from believing in God to definitely believing in Christ—in Christianity."[11] At the age of thirty-one, the years of struggle ended. In his book, *Surprised by Joy* (1955) Lewis wrote about his spiritual journey from atheism to Christianity. He felt there was simply no choice but to believe in God. When he truly knew that Jesus was his Savior, there was no mediocrity—he became passionate about his beliefs. Lewis once said: "I believe in Christianity as I believe that the sun has risen: not only because I see it, but because by it I see everything else."

C.S. LEWIS—PASSIONATE WRITER

Once C.S. Lewis became a Christian, it was as if his purpose in life, which was writing, ignited with his passion for the Lord. As the years followed, Lewis published more than thirty magnificent books. He wrote in a wide variety of genres. Nearly anyone could find something they would like from among the works of C.S. Lewis. He wrote poetry, science fiction, fantasy, and books defending the Christian faith. He could write about the gospel so anyone could understand, going directly to the heart of the matter.

A mere sampling of his genius in writing includes the following. His first major book was *The Pilgrim's Regress* (1933), which is about his discovery of the Christian faith. *The Screwtape Letters* (1942) is a very innovative and popular book about a series of letters from Screwtape, a demonic tempter, and a junior tempter on his first assignment with temptation.

According to an article by Dr. David R. Reagan, Lewis' *Mere Christianity* (1952) "has been the number one best selling Christian book since World War II."[12] This book discloses Lewis' Christian beliefs, which were written from a series of radio broadcasts he delivered over the BBC. When these broadcasts were given, it was to British citizens huddling in bomb shelters during the war. While contemplating whether they would survive the night, Lewis gave them a hope founded on solid truth.

As World War II continued, Lewis then living in a huge house (called the Kilns) with eight acres in rural England, offered to take some children (evacuees) to live with him. They loved where he lived in the countryside and they adored the animals, but they always seemed to want something to do. The thought occurred to Lewis to write a book for children. Ever since his teenage years, he had been thinking about writing a story with animals. "So far, all he had was the image of a faun with an umbrella walking through a snowy wood. That was as far as it ever got."[13] One day he knew exactly where the story was to take place and who the characters would be. After finishing the first chapter, he read it to the children, who were his first critics. After their inspiring comments, he began writing the first book in the now famous series.

The Chronicles of Narnia have been his most popular books (published from 1950-1956) but were not well received at first. "Initially, when Lewis turned to writing children's books, his publisher and some of his friends tried to dissuade him; they thought it would hurt his reputation as a writer of serious works. J.R.R. Tolkien in particular criticized Lewis' first Narnia book, *The Lion, the Witch and the Wardrobe*. He thought that there were too many elements that clashed—a Father Christmas *and* an evil witch, talking animals *and* children. Thankfully, Lewis didn't listen to any of them."[14] Lewis decided to proceed with publishing his book, knowing he was born to do this. Because he followed his heart and published the series of seven books, they have become some of the most beloved classics of children's literature.

In Lewis we have a good example of how to proceed toward doing what we believe is God's will, regardless of what others may think, even our close friends. This is not to say that we should not listen to our friends, because guidance from others can be helpful. Even so, we cannot let what even our closest friends say eclipse what we know in our own hearts. Sometimes, the road to victory may be a lonely one, which is intended to draw us even closer to the Lord.

On a side note, Lewis had been corresponding with an American woman named Joy Gresham. She was a single mother with two boys and she was also an author.

He was in need of a secretary and she was in need of work, so Lewis offered her a job and she moved to England to work for him. However, her visa was soon denied. The only solution to help her to stay in England in Lewis' mind was to marry her. In 1956 they decided to marry, even though they both knew it was a loveless marriage.

But when she was diagnosed with bone cancer in 1957 and she was close to dying, "it was at this point that Lewis realized just how much he loved her. In March of 1957, the two were married again, this time by an Anglican priest, in a bedside ceremony at the hospital."[15] Lewis prayed continually for her and, amazingly, she did go into remission. They felt this time was a gift from the Lord and they used it to the fullest. However, at the same time Lewis' joints were hurting and he had some tests done that confirmed, ironically, that he was suffering from a chronic bone disease. They were able to travel to Ireland and later to Greece, but at times both of them were hobbling, as Joy was no longer in remission with the cancer. Sadly, the marriage only lasted four years because of Joy's death in 1960. To have found love toward the end of their lives was an unexpected blessing for both C.S. Lewis and Joy. He told Joy before she died that he would take care of her boys. And true to his word, he did.

Lewis published very few books after his wife's death. However, one amazing book, *The Four Loves,* was published in 1960, the year Joy died. In this book, Lewis discusses the nature of the different types of love: affection, friendship, Eros (romantic love), and charity. Perhaps finally discovering love in his own life enabled him to expound even more on the extensive subject of love in such a heart-rending way.

C.S. Lewis passed away on Friday, November 22, 1963. He may be physically gone, but his legacy will live on through his many writings for generations to come. C.S. Lewis' power in writing came from a passion from what he knew to be true. He had a gift and he used it to the fullest. His writings have helped millions of people find a closer walk with God. Charles Colson, who served as Special Counsel to U.S. President Richard Nixon and is the founder of Prison Fellowship Ministries said this well: "Lewis exhorted Christians to get ready for the Second Coming simply by staying at our post, faithfully doing whatever we are called to do. And when we do, God will often use our efforts in ways we cannot imagine. The God of whom C.S. Lewis wrote so movingly is still sovereign, and still surprises us with the way He works through humble human instruments—if only we are faithful."[16] Lewis was indeed faithful in his purpose; we can do the same.

PASSION IN WRITING

Excitement exists in the very being of those who are passionate in their purpose. Wherever they go, people can feel their enthusiasm. Those who are passionate in what they believe seem to have endless energy, while pushing forward with a commitment to make their dreams come true.

A writer, for example, must be passionate with his words. Otherwise, his words will have no meaning. One time I asked a friend if he thought he would ever write a book. His reply was: "Yes, if I have something worth saying." How true his statement is. If writers are just writing words with no passion, the words are meaningless. How will it affect anyone? To be passionate in writing means that there is an extreme or intense enthusiasm to write in words what the heart is saying.

Have you ever read a book and the words immediately went straight to your heart and stayed there? That writer's passion for his subject ignited the passion within you and then you became intensely enthusiastic over the subject. The key to writing this way is to write when the passion is lit. The same is true with any purpose. We must fulfill what we have been called to do when our passion is ignited. And, when the fire is blazing, we must never let the flame be extinguished.

The power of passion ignites the fire of creativity, as we have seen in Lewis' life. May we be inspired by his story—finding the truth in all things passionately, while following our hearts to fulfill our purpose in life.

Our passions are not too strong, they are too weak.
We are far too easily pleased.
~ C.S. Lewis

CHAPTER THREE

THE POWER OF DEVOTION

MARIE CURIE'S UNWAVERING DEVOTION

Life is not easy for any of us. But what of that? We must
have perseverance...We must believe we are gifted for
something and that this thing must be attained.
~Marie Curie

Those who accomplish great things in life are devoted to their purpose with passion, and nothing deters them from finishing their goals. Marya Sklodowska, better known as Marie Curie, was just such a woman. Her extreme devotion to science began when her sister, Zosia, died at an early age, and later when her mother died of tuberculosis when Marie was only nine years old.

Marie Curie became the first woman in Europe to receive a doctorate and the first person to receive two Nobel Prizes in a lifetime. She faced tragedy in life, suffered a miscarriage, and lost her husband, yet prevailed, never losing sight of her many goals. She was in a world that few women had ever dared to enter. And, no matter what she faced, she found a way to push through to victory. She is an example to us all that with the power of devotion, amazing things will happen. "Marie Curie is considered by most to be the greatest woman scientist of all time."[1] But, as we will learn, there is usually a price to pay for advancement. This is her story.

MARYA, THE STUDENT

Marya was born in Warsaw, Poland on November 7, 1867. Her family was educated and cultured, but struggled financially. She was an excellent student and, even at a young age, loved science and mathematics, graduating at the top of her class at fifteen. Women were not permitted to receive advanced degrees in Poland at the time, but this was her dream and she would not let it die. To pay for the college tuition at the Sorbonne in Paris, where she wanted to attend college, she became a governess and tutor for eight years, working hard to earn the money for school. She not only saved money for her education, but she helped pay for medical school tuition in Paris for her sister Bronya, who became a medical doctor in 1891.

Marie's education came at the cost of years in her life, not only to earn the money to pay for her education, but the years of being trained in her field. But those years were not wasted—far from it. If she had not been focused and diligent to be trained, she would never have been able to succeed in accomplishing her goals. This we need to understand as well. It is so easy to want to plow ahead once we know what our purpose in life is, but we will never accomplish the totality of our purpose by doing this prematurely. We must take the time to be trained.

Bronya married another medical student who became a doctor as well, and they were able to begin their practice in Paris. To help Marya fulfill her dream of a college education, they invited her to come live with them, which enabled her to save more money for her education by not having to rent a place to live. Soon after earning the needed money to attend college, Marya registered at the age of twenty-four at the Sorbonne (now the Universities of Paris) in 1891, under the French version of her first name, "Marie." Her obsession was to learn and that she did, graduating first in her class in 1893 in physics and mathematics. She also attained a master's degree in both subjects a year later.

MARIE CURIE, SCIENTIST AND NOBEL PRIZE WINNER

Marie had met a highly acclaimed professor at the School of Physics named Pierre Curie. He wrote to her saying how nice it would be to "spend life side-by-side, in the sway of our dreams: your patriotic dream, our humanitarian dream and our scientific dream."[2] She married Pierre on July 26, 1895, thus beginning an extraordinary partnership in scientific history.

Pierre and Marie were inseparable, always working together in a laboratory during the day and studying together at night. They were blessed with two daughters, Irene, born 1897, and Eve, born in 1904. Marie also miscarried a baby, later discovering that it was probably due to the extreme amount of radiation she was exposed to daily. Thankfully, Pierre's father helped to take care of the children as Marie and Pierre became more and more involved in their work.

Marie wanted to pursue a doctorate in physics. For her thesis, she chose to study the source of the mysterious, invisible energy of X-rays discovered by German physicists, Wilhelm Roentgen and Henri Becquerel, who had discovered that uranium salts emitted comparable radiation. With Pierre advising her, Marie spent several years purifying several tons of uranium ore. She worked outdoors in a drafty shed, which had some circulation of air. This was a blessing due to the fact she was being exposed to poisonous radon gas, of which the Curies were totally unaware.

During their research, Marie and Pierre coined the word "radioactive." They discovered that the rays resulted when something happened within the atom itself. They uncovered two radioactive elements— "polonium," named in honor of Marie's native Poland, and "radium," the stronger of the two radioactive elements, named after the radiant blue light it emitted. In 1902, they isolated enough radium to substantiate its existence, earning Marie a doctorate in physics. She was the first woman in Europe to achieve a doctorate.

Becquerel and the Curies were awarded the 1903 Nobel Prize in Physics for their combined discovery of natural radioactivity. This was no small feat as Marie was the first woman to ever receive a Nobel Prize.

TRAGEDY STRIKES

But their happiness was momentary. Here was another cost to be paid—they did not know at the time the radioactive substances, which they handled bare-handed were dangerous. They often kept the radioactive material that emitted a blue light by their bedside or in their pockets because they loved their work so much. "Even to this day, the notebooks used by the Curies to record their work, are radioactive, and will continue to be so for a long time, as the half-life of radium is 1,620 years!"[3]

In 1906, because of Pierre's radiation exposure, he was in a weakened state and was tragically killed by a horse-drawn carriage while attempting to cross the street. Marie was hurt over the loss of her husband, yet she still remained focused, even through this tragedy. She was now a single mother who educated her two daughters and took on the position of professor that her husband had acquired at the Sorbonne, becoming the first woman professor there.

Marie spent most of her time in her laboratory. She determined the atomic weight of radium, and amazingly received a second Nobel Prize in 1911—this one in chemistry. She became the first person to receive two Nobel Prizes in a lifetime.

Madame Curie, a Humanitarian

When World War I began, she said, "we must act" as "her real joy was easing human suffering."[4] Marie felt that X-rays could be of use in locating shrapnel and bullets in soldiers, enabling the wounded to receive immediate treatment with surgery. Because of her devotion to mankind, she helped fit X-ray machines in vans to be used on the battlefield, personally driving a van herself to the frontlines. Marie was accompanied by her daughter, Irene, risking their own lives to help save others. Marie taught operators to use the machines and established permanent X-ray units in hospitals throughout France and Belgium. Marie was exhausted, but she had won a place in the hearts of the French people.

After the war ended, Marie began raising funds for a hospital and laboratory devoted to radiology. In 1921, Marie was invited to tour the United States to let others know about her project. When she left America she had enough money, equipment, and radium to begin her new laboratory. She toured a second time and raised even more money for the Radium Institute. "In 1929, President Hoover of the United States presented her with a gift of $50,000, donated by American friends of science, to purchase radium for use in the laboratory in Warsaw."[5] She controlled the largest supply of radioactive substances used in scientific research for studying the structure of the atom. Working together harmoniously, Dr. Claudius Regaud headed the biology laboratory while Marie headed the research laboratory. "During her work, Marie discovered radiation could kill human cells. She reasoned that if it could kill healthy human cells, it could kill diseased human cells and went about isolating radium for use in killing tumors."[6] Radium was provided by physicists and chemists; then the physicians used it to treat cancer patients.

Those working with her in her lab became sick with fatigue, burns, and some were even dying young due to cancer from radiation exposure. Marie had been exposed to incredible amounts of radium, and it was hard for her to admit that the element she and her husband had

discovered and loved so much could be at fault. She thought only of the potential it had to heal people. "The work she did, she did with patience, often getting results only after years of careful experimentation, while struggling for money to support her work."[7] Eventually though, she did accept the fact that radium was dangerous. Still, she continued on with her work with great stamina.

Sadly though, in the last decade of her life, Marie's health began to worsen with dizziness, aches, and pains, just as her husband Pierre had suffered. She began having fever, ringing in her ears, and gradual loss of eyesight. She died on July 4, 1934 at the age of sixty-seven from leukemia caused by the effects of radiation exposure. The cost was great, but because of the devotion to her research, many others' lives were saved with radiation treatments for cancer. "The work of Marie Curie was not just important for her discoveries of new elements, but the process she used to isolate them helped to create a "stockpile" of a few grams of radioactive material, which future scientists could use for further studies. As a result of her work, X-rays are very common today, as is carbon dating, radiotherapy, and other medical applications for radiation."[8] She paid a high price for such an achievement, but in doing so, she has helped to prolong the lives of countless people. Value cannot be placed on such an accomplishment.

MADAME CURIE'S LEGACY

Madame Curie trained Irene, her daughter, to be a physicist as well, thereby passing on her purpose as a legacy to her daughter, and later to her granddaughter, Helene. Irene married Frederic Joliot, and they succeeded

Madame Curie as directors at the Radium Institute (later renamed the Curie Institute). Irene and Frederic were awarded the Nobel Prize in Chemistry for their discovery of artificial radioactivity in 1935. Marie was the first woman to receive a Nobel Prize and have a daughter to receive one as well. Marie's daughter, Eve married Henry R. Labouisse, an American diplomat, who received a Nobel Prize for Peace in 1965 on behalf of UNICEF. Marie's granddaughter, Dr. Helene Langevin-Joliot, also worked in the field of radioactivity and was a Professor of Nuclear Physics and Chemistry at the University of Paris. Incredibly, together, the Curie/Joliot/Labouisee family won four Nobel prizes.

> *The contributions that Marie Curie made to science are immense. With her help, doctors have been able to treat cancer, manipulate nuclear energy, create atomic bombs, and numerous other achievements have stemmed from her work. Giving of her time, energy and, ultimately, her life, Marie Curie's work continues through scientists around the world as they build upon her basic foundation to discover more in the areas of science and mathematics.*[9]

THE POWER OF DEVOTION

We can learn much from the power of Madame Curie's devotion of her purpose. She was completely devoted to her research throughout her life. Many of her evenings were spent in research, which meant she gave up most of her leisure time. She was known to have the constitution of a horse, never seeming to tire. Because of her willingness to persevere, while remaining devoted to her goal in the study of radium, hundreds of thousands have benefited from her efforts. "To this end, in 1914 she helped found the Pasteur Institute and the Radium Institute in Paris, whose laboratories are used to conduct research that finds ways to use radiation to diagnose and treat cancer. In addition to her scientific achievements, Marie Curie was a humanitarian who wished to use all her knowledge and research for the good of mankind."[10]

Those who have accomplished great things are powerfully devoted with vision and passion—nothing deters them from their purpose in life. This kind of devotion does not know the meaning of the word "fail."

Marie and Pierre Curie both died from exposure to radium, but Pierre did not know the effects of radium. Marie did. Yet her devotion did not waver and she kept pushing forward. Marie's life was not devoted to herself—she was devoted to science and others. Because of her research, many people with cancer lived longer lives than would have been possible. Devotion means sacrifice, but it also means success.

I never see what has been done;
I only see what remains to be done.
~Marie Curie

CHAPTER FOUR

THE POWER OF PERSEVERANCE

JIM VALVANO, A MAN WHO FULFILLED HIS DREAMS

How do you go from where you are to where
you want to be? I think you have to have an
enthusiasm for life. You have to have a dream,
a goal. You have to be willing to work for it.
~Jim Valvano

With the power of perseverance, a goal will be completed, and such was the miraculous case with Jim Valvano and the North Carolina State University basketball team (the Wolfpack) more than twenty years ago. Basketball is only a game, but the principles the Wolfpack used in this miraculous 1983 ACC and NCAA Tournament season may be applied to any goal. From this true story we will learn how Jim Valvano, the North Carolina State basketball coach, and his team powerfully worked with passion and perseverance, making a dream come true. Even today, coaches use what happened that year with the North Carolina State basketball team as an inspirational story for their teams. Indeed, a true legacy was left behind.

North Carolina State University, Duke University, and the University of North Carolina (UNC) are within miles of each other. They are all rivals, making basketball all the more fun and exciting in North Carolina.

The year 1983 is huge in my memory as I was working at N.C. State and taking several English classes there. I will never forget the excitement at N.C. State that year. Here is the story.

JIM VALVANO

Jim Valvano was a man of vision and passion. With his positive coaching skills, he encouraged his team to never let their dreams die. Few men in the coaching field have before or since had his zest and enthusiasm for coaching. This passion began at an early age.

"Legend has it that when Valvano was seventeen, he scrawled his lifelong ambitions on a simple white index card. Included on this card were:

1) Play high school and college basketball.

2) Become an assistant, then head college basketball coach.

3) Achieve a victory in Madison Square Garden.

4) Cut down the nets after winning a national championship.

It took the man with a heart dwarfed only by his dreams all of nineteen years to accomplish it all. And when he did, he still had the index card."[1] At thirty-six years old, these were amazing achievements.

Writing down goals is an excellent idea. By placing them in a visible spot, they will be seen daily. With perseverance and hard work, our goals will be achieved. As we never lose sight of them, we can achieve great things just as we will learn that Jimmy Valvano and his N.C. State basketball team did in 1983.

As a background, it would be helpful to learn some of what the man, Jim Valvano, was like. He was a comedian, very charismatic, and well-liked by all. At a press conference, "Valvano asked reporters if they knew what the N.C. State dental plan was. When the reporters all shrugged, he said, 'We either win or the alumni bash out our teeth!'"[2]

At another time he said,

> I asked a ref if he could give me a technical foul for thinking bad things about him. He said, "Of course not." I said, "Well, I think you stink." And he gave me a technical. You can't trust 'em.

Once when N.C. State lost to UNC, Valvano told reporters, "This fellow wrote me that if we lose one more game to North Carolina (UNC), he's going to come up and shoot my dog. I wrote him back that I appreciated his interest but I didn't have a dog. A couple days later, the guy sends me a dog!"[3]

Valvano kept this kind of comedy going, winning the hearts of the press and fans. He had seemingly endless energy, pushing forward constantly to make his dreams come true. He also was a great coach.

In *Three Paths to Glory,* Barry Jacobs wrote this about Valvano:

> For him, then and now, the game's the thing. The game, and winning. Show Valvano a game and he'll try to master it, to learn the limits and figure a way to beat them.
>
> He's no system guy, trying to force you to do things his way. He's a counter puncher, adaptable, reading what exists rather than trying to impose order.
>
> Nor was Valvano ever content with being simply a coach. He knew he didn't have to be, given his glib tongue, comic's timing, and a mind that dances like a water sprite. To be around him is to be endlessly entertained, to feel good. He's fun; the rare person who can make you think and laugh at the same time. It's an attractive quality, and marketable in any realm, especially recruiting. Join me, he told youngsters. Play for me, win with me.[4]

Valvano was an amazing man who loved the game of basketball. And, he loved his team.

1983 ACC TOURNAMENT

The two most talented teams in the Atlantic Coast Conference (ACC) that year were UNC and Virginia. Even Wake Forest had a better record than N.C. State. Most did not even look twice at N.C. State, largely due to an injury to one of their key players, Dereck Whittenburg, a shooting guard who missed twelve games that season. But with two games left, Whittenburg returned and was ready to play. However, N.C. State still ended the season with a mediocre record of 17-10.

Valvano felt they had to win the ACC tournament to get a bid to play in the NCAA tournament. He encouraged his team to keep their dream alive to win, and they did. N.C. State beat Wake Forest in the first round. Next they played their all-time rival UNC, winning in overtime! Relief washed over the Wolfpack—they had made it to the championship game. But this was no time to relax in the glow of victory for they were about to play Virginia, the team who had the best college record in the last four years due to Ralph Sampson, three-time NCAA player of the year. Amazingly though, against all odds, N.C. State rallied from an eight-point deficit and won by three points, earning them the title of ACC Champions of 1983! This gave them a place in the NCAA Tournament. One dream had finally come true.

NCAA Tournament

Fifty-two teams competed in the 1983 NCAA Tournament that year. Of course, odds were that the most talented team would win. However, after winning the ACC Tournament, Valvano and his team believed anything was possible! He kept telling them to: "Never give up your dreams!" Over and over he told his team to reach higher. Deep down inside they knew they had the talent to win.

Game 1: N.C. State Against Pepperdine

Valvano continued using a fouling strategy that proved to be an asset in his games. His team would foul the other team's least talented free throw shooters, hoping they would miss, giving the ball back to N.C. State. To their advantage, it worked most of the time.

N.C. State beat Pepperdine and won 69-67 in double overtime! This was when the Wolfpack was tagged the "THE TEAM OF DESTINY." Something struck the heart of the Wolfpack when they heard that, giving them even more vision and diligence to keep pushing forward.

GAME 2: N.C. STATE AGAINST UNLV

An amazing game! With N.C. State's final possession trailing, 69-70, and three seconds left, Thurl Bailey, a forward, threw an off balance shot and won the game! The excitement in their hometown of Raleigh began to rise—most could not wait to see what this "Team of Destiny" would do next.

GAME 3: N.C. STATE AGAINST BOSTON COLLEGE

There were sixteen teams remaining—all battling to become champion. The game with Boston College proved to be their easiest. A very happy Wolfpack shot 79 percent in the second half to win 75-56. They would need this type of encouragement since their next game would be far different. They would have to play Virginia again, who still remained one of the favorites to win the NCAA championship. But Valvano never stopped encouraging his team to believe in themselves. They had beaten Virginia once, and they could do it again.

GAME 4: N.C. STATE AGAINST VIRGINIA

This would be the third time N.C. State would meet Virginia that season, so they knew what they were up against. The Wolfpack played hard and was able to keep the score tied with only one minute left to play. They fouled Othell Wilson, a fair Virginia free throw shooter, and he made one of the free throws. Virginia led by one (62-61). Lorenzo Charles, one of N.C. State's forwards was fouled. He hit both free throws, winning the game. The Wolfpack was on their way to the Final Four!

After this game, they began receiving nicknames like: "The Cinderella Team," "Destiny's Darlings," "The Kardiac Kids," and "The Cardiac Pack," all of which were very appropriate names. Every game kept you on the edge of your seat, making you wonder if your heart could take another minute!

The team flew back to Raleigh to practice, and four thousand enthusiastic fans showed up to watch them. When they left on a bus to catch their flight to Albuquerque, where the NCAA championship was to be played, fans lined the interstate to wish them well. It was an amazing time in basketball history.

ALBUQUERQUE—THE FINAL FOUR, N.C. STATE AGAINST GEORGIA

The biggest topic in Albuquerque was Jim Valvano's Cinderella Team. Could the Wolfpack really pull this off and win the championship? Valvano knew they could, and he encouraged his players to be open and talk with the press. In turn the press wrote encouraging stories about them.

Georgia had never been to the Final Four and they desperately wanted to win. The "Team of Destiny," however, had other ideas—they wanted to see their dream come true. In this game, N.C. State never lost control of the ball and they won 67-60. The upcoming championship game would not be so easy—it was to be their biggest challenge yet.

THE NCAA CHAMPIONSHIP GAME— N.C. STATE AGAINST HOUSTON

N.C. State was not playing against just any team— they were playing against Houston, who was seemingly unbeatable. This is what *The Washington Post's* Dave Kindred wrote:

> *Trees will tap dance, elephants will ride in the Indianapolis 500 and Orson Welles will skip breakfast, lunch, and dinner before State finds a way to beat Houston![5]*

Later, Valvano put that quote on his office wall. As much as they were liked, few were giving N.C. State a chance to win. The experts were saying the matchup was like David against Goliath. N.C. State could have actually taken that as encouragement because as most know, David won his battle against Goliath!

Valvano and his team were still believing that anything was possible. At half-time they were ahead 33-25, and were feeling quite good about their performance. However, Houston came out after half-time with a vengeance and outscored N.C. State in the first ten minutes, taking a 42-35 lead. Most thought the game was over— but it was far from over. Houston's coach, "Guy Lewis inexplicably slowed down the pace of the game, and that played into the hands of the underdog N.C. State team...it ultimately cost them down the stretch when State began to employ its press-and-foul maneuver. The Wolfpack scratched its way back into a 52-52 tie with just over a minute remaining."[6]

One of the most thrilling and heart-stopping finishes in NCAA history was about to happen in the next forty-four seconds! N.C. State had the ball; N.C. State's Bailey threw it to Whittenburg, who held onto the ball, desperately looking for a final shot. Only a few seconds remained on the clock. With urgency, he threw a thirty footer, missing. Houston did not see the ball falling short, but N.C. State's Lorenzo Charles did. He grabbed it in midair and threw it in the basket as the final horn sounded! I will never forget that moment as the basketball landed in the hoop. The stadium went wild and everyone on the N.C. State team was jumping, running, and hugging anybody and everybody!

Christopher Young wrote about this exciting moment in NCAA history.

> *It was good! The game was over! And North Carolina State had stunned the college-basketball universe with a 54-52 last-second victory over the Goliath-like Houston Cougars. Famous footage from those frantic few seconds after the winning dunk show the euphoric Valvano running around the court in search of someone to hug, ultimately settling on 65-year-old N.C. State athletic director Willis Casey.*[7]

Christopher Young also wrote: "Whatever Valvano's legacy is, his 1983 club's miracle run to the NCAA championship remains an inspiration to teams everywhere...."[8]

According to Mike Towle in *I Remember Jim Valvano,* "While that Cinderella story was Valvano's only national championship, he quickly came to symbolize the exuberance and excellence of the exciting world of college basketball. Valvano transcended his sport, touching millions as he emerged as one of the most charismatic and ultimately courageous figures in American life...Valvano's life is the classic story of courage and determination as born out in his memorable line: 'Don't give up. Don't ever give up!'"[9]

VALVANO'S LEGACY

In the years following the 1983 NCAA championship, Valvano faced some charges that seemed unbelievable to those who knew him. Valvano's image became tarnished by the accusations in his basketball program, and he insisted they were not true to the very end. Then the unthinkable happened. In 1990, Jim Valvano was fired as head basketball coach at N.C. State. Reportedly, it was not due to an investigation by the NCAA, but most likely from the internal and external perception that some had of the program. Regardless, his contributions to the N.C. State basketball program and basketball in general cannot be taken away—nor will the memories of that incredible 1983 NCAA basketball tournament be forgotten. He brought new life, excitement, and fun to basketball, and for that he should be well remembered.

He did not let losing his job stop him from moving forward in life—not Jim Valvano. He soon began a new career as a colorful ESPN college basketball commentator. And in 1992, because he was so good at being a commentator, and true to his "never give up" attitude, he won an ACE (Award of Cable Television) for Best Sports Commentator/Analyst.

In 1992, Valvano began fighting another battle—a battle for his life. "...True to his personality, he did not let the illness keep him down. Instead, in his final year he established the V Foundation (www.jimmyv.org), which raises funds for cancer research."[10] At the 1993 ESPY awards, which was fifty-five days before his death, Valvano received the Arthur Ashe Courage and Humanitarian Award. "A few weeks before he died, he was honored on national television and to that vast viewing audience, he said this:

> Today I fight a different battle. You see...cancer is attacking and destroying my body, but what cancer cannot touch is my mind, my heart, and my soul. I have faith in God and hope that things might get better for me. But even if they don't, I promise you this: I will never, ever give up. And if cancer gets me, then I'll just try my best to go to heaven...to be the best coach they've ever seen up there. Then he pointed to his 1983 championship team, I learned a great lesson from these guys. They amazed me. They did things I was not sure they could do because they absolutely refused to give up. That was the theme of our championship season: "Never, ever give up!' That's the lesson I learned from them, and that's the message I leave with you. Never give up. Never, ever give up!"[11]

If a dying man could still have this kind of courage and enthusiasm, how much more should we who are living and have time to fulfill that which we were born to do?

Valvano accomplished some amazing things in his life. In his ten seasons at N.C. State, he appeared in eight NCAA tournaments and won the miraculous 1983 NCAA Championship. He also won two ACC tournament championships. These are astonishing achievements in the conference that is arguably the best in the country, and often fields at least six of the top twenty teams in the country. He was ACC Coach of the Year twice, and had a winning career record of 346-212.

Along with his incredible achievements previously mentioned, Valvano was inducted into the Rutgers Basketball Hall of Fame in April 1993, into the Rutgers Hall of Distinguished Alumni in May1999, and into New York City's Basketball Hall of Fame in September1999.

Though it would have been easy to give up after Valvano was fired, he did not. He stood up and began a whole new career of being a commentator. This setback actually propelled him forward into something new and fresh. Though he did not live long after he began this new career, he clearly demonstrated his true character. There are times when we may face an experience such as being fired or some other type of rejection in our work, but part of our training in fulfilling that which we have been called to do is to rise up when we are down. Jim Valvano was a great example of what will happen when perseverance is part of who we are.

When we have the power of passion and perseverance in what God has called us to do, we can pass it on. Valvano imparted his own passion to his championship team. Following their coach's continual encouragement, they chose to never give up. We have the greatest Coach of all, and His Words are always a source of encouragement.

Let us not forget that the passion within us is what ignites the passion in others. To become a great basketball player requires the perseverance to work and practice endless hours at perfecting skills while coming up with new strategies. Having this kind of perseverance will likewise enable us to fulfill our own purpose in life. Our hearts must never let go of our dreams. Just like with the N.C. State basketball team, our purpose in life may seem far beyond what we think we can do. But remember this: God would not have given us such a purpose if we could not do it—there is always a way!

Do not let another day go by without working toward fulfilling what you were born to do. You will never regret the time it will take to make your dreams come true. Remember a dream is merely a dream unless you do something about it. Perseverance and hard work powerfully combined with passion will make dreams become reality. Jim Valvano and his N.C. State team proved in 1983 that dreams can come true.

To get where you've never been,
you have to do what you've never done....
~Jim Valvano

CHAPTER FIVE

THE POWER OF FOCUS

THE BRILLIANCE OF THOMAS EDISON

The best thinking
has been done in solitude.
~ Thomas Edison

Focus and concentration work together. Focus is the power that lights the way to clearly see ahead, enabling us to set goals and accomplish them. Having concentration will give us the ability to work toward the goal no matter how long it takes to finish it.

A MAN WHO FULFILLED HIS DESTINY

Thomas Alva Edison's story is quite inspirational and should give us hope that we can accomplish in life what the Lord has given us to do, for Edison did indeed fulfill his destiny.

I never failed once. It just happened to be a 2000-step process.

                               ~Thomas Edison

Thomas Edison responded to a reporter with the above quote after he had failed two thousand times before he successfully invented the light bulb. As his life portrayed, he knew the meaning of the words "focus."

Thomas Alva Edison was born on February 11, 1847. Although, he did not learn to talk until he was almost four years old, he made up for lost time when he finally began to communicate. He wanted to know how everything worked. His persistent questioning in school was not appreciated by his teacher, so his mother withdrew Thomas at the age of seven from school to "home-teach" him. Basically, he had only three months of formal education. His mother taught Edison the "three R's" (reading, writing, and arithmetic) as well as the Bible. Evidently, Bible training stayed with him all of his life when he later made the following comment about religious training:

Religious beliefs implanted in childhood stay with the adult in spite of everything. It is necessary to take them young and to teach morality and character...

By age twelve, Thomas was essentially an adult. He started his own business by selling newspapers and snacks on the railroad, and fruits and vegetables in town. Being the resourceful young man that he was, at age fourteen he began his own newspaper, *The Weekly Herald.* At its peak, this newspaper was selling four hundred copies a day.

THE POWER OF FOCUS

Thomas loved to experiment and he kept some of his chemicals in the back of one of the train's baggage cars. One day the train lurched, causing a stick of phosphorous to ignite and the baggage car to catch fire. The conductor was outraged with Thomas and struck him powerfully on the side of his head, which some have suggested began his hearing loss.

Thomas contracted scarlet fever when he was fourteen, which may have eventually caused him to become totally deaf in his left ear and approximately 80 percent in his right ear. But instead of being detoured from his potential in life, he used the hearing loss to greatly enhance the power of his concentration and focus. He realized these were the keys to success in any endeavor. "Not long after he had acquired the means to have an operation that 'would have most likely restored his hearing,' he flatly refused to act upon the option. His rationale was that he was afraid he 'would have difficulty re-learning how to channel his thinking in an ever more noisy world.'"[1]

We could learn from his example as well. Though we certainly do not want to become deaf to learn such a lesson, we must learn to use the gift of focus for what it is. The more we are focused, the more clearly and sharply defined our vision will be.

Because of his hearing loss, he was prevented from receiving secondary education in contemporary mathematics, physics, and engineering. But he did not allow this to stop him from finding other ways to learn.

When I want to discover something, I begin by reading up everything that has been done along that line in the past—that's what all these books in the library are for. I see what has been accomplished at great labor and expense in the past. I gather the data of many thousands of experiments as a starting point, and then I make thousands more.

~Thomas Edison

THOMAS EDISON, THE INVENTOR

One day Thomas happened to see the station master's young son wander onto the tracks in front of an oncoming train. He jumped on the train tracks and rescued the young boy. Because of this, the boy's grateful father taught him how to use Morse Code and the telegraph. At age fifteen, Thomas had mastered the basics and began a career as a telegraph operator. As he enhanced his speed and efficiency, he experimented to improve the device.

At age sixteen he set off on his own. "After working in a variety of telegraph offices...he finally came up with his first authentic invention. Called an 'automatic repeater,' it transmitted telegraph signals between unmanned stations, allowing virtually anyone to easily and accurately translate code at their own speed and convenience."[2]

While working as a telegraph operator, he met an associate of Alexander Graham Bell's named Benjamin Franklin Bredding, who was more knowledgeable than Bell or himself with telegraphy and electricity. This relationship would prove significant later in life.

From this point on in Edison's life, his genius began to blossom. In 1868, he came up with his first patented invention, an Electrical Vote Recorder.

In 1869, while seeking work in New York City, he wandered into the operating room of the Gold & Stock Telegraph Company where he noticed their ticker apparatus was broken down. He repaired it (no one had been able to) and was given the remarkable wage of $300 a month as a job superintendent. While there he radically improved stock tickers. In 1870, he patented his next invention, the Universal Stock Ticker and Unison Device, and he received his first cash payment for all the rights to this invention: $40,000! He was then able to help his parents who were struggling financially.

From 1872-1878, Edison patented several of his most important inventions, including the motograph and automatic telegraph systems which saved *Western Union* millions of dollars in wiring. He also invented paraffin paper (used to wrap candles), the electric pen (forerunner of a mimeograph machine), and his favorite invention, the first phonograph in 1877.

In 1879, Alexander Graham Bell beat him in the race to patent the first authentic transmission of the human voice. Edison had been working on the carbon transmitter, which ultimately made Bell's amazing telephone audible for practical use. But later in 1879, Edison beat all of his competition by inventing the first commercially practical light bulb!

That was not enough for Thomas Edison. He came up with the invention which had more impact than any other invention at that time. "In 1883 and 1884, while beating a path from his research lab to the patent office, he introduced the world's first economically viable system of centrally generating and distributing electric light, heat, and power."[3] Even his critics granted him that this was a phenomenal achievement.

"By 1887, Edison was recognized for having set up the world's first full-fledged research and development center in West Orange, New Jersey...Within a year, this fantastic operation was the largest scientific testing laboratory in the world."[4]

Another popular invention of Edison's was the Vitascope, which would eventually lead to silent motion pictures. Then in 1892, Edison General Electric Company began with another firm and became known as the famous General Electric Corporation.

Edison's inventions are too numerous to mention all of them here. The power of his focus in fulfilling his goals was amazing. By the age of eighty-three, he had obtained 1,093 patents, averaging a new patent every two weeks throughout his working career. "Accordingly, many serious science and technology historians grant that he was indeed 'the most influential figure of our millennium.'"[5]

Thomas Edison saw huge changes happen in his lifetime—many were because of him. He was able to take his ideas and make them a reality. He understood well that everyone has unique gifts, but many never discover what they are.

Every man has some forte, something he can do better than he can do anything else. Many men, however, never find the job they are best suited for. And often this is because they do not think enough. Too many men drift lazily into any job, suited or unsuited for them; and when they don't get along well they blame everybody and everything but themselves.

~Thomas Edison

He set a fine example to follow. He never made excuses and he did not stop until he accomplished what he set out to do. Edison said, "I never did anything by accident, nor did any of my inventions come by accident; they came by work."

SATISFACTION IN WORK

Solomon, one of the wisest of men, wrote the book of Ecclesiastes, which is basically about experiences in life. In Ecclesiastes 2:24-26, he wrote about the things he enjoyed: food, drink, and the satisfaction in *work*. Work, you might say—how can anyone enjoy work?

> **So I decided there is nothing better than to enjoy food and drink and *to find satisfaction in work*. Then I realized that this pleasure is from the hand of God.**
>
> **For who can eat or enjoy anything apart from him?**
>
> **God gives wisdom, knowledge, and joy to those who please him... (NLT).**

The word "work" can bring many thoughts to mind, most of which are not pleasant. But here Solomon says **"there is nothing better than to enjoy food and drink and *to find satisfaction in work.*"** I believe this is true. We all love to eat good food as he mentions—that is a pleasant thought. But he also mentions the satisfaction that comes from work *and* enjoying food and drink in the same sentence. Solomon said that **"this pleasure is from the hand of God."** It feels good to complete a goal, and we feel a sense of satisfaction. However, to accomplish something of worth is work!

*I find my greatest pleasure, and so my reward, in
the work that precedes what the world calls success.*

~Thomas Edison

THE PLEASURE OF WORK

In the book of Proverbs, Solomon also enlightens us
on the work skills of an ant, such a tiny creature.

**Go to the ant, O sluggard, Observe her ways
and be wise,**

Which, having no chief, officer or ruler,

**Prepares her food in the summer and gathers
her provision in the harvest.**

**How long will you lie down, O sluggard? When
will you arise from your sleep?**

**"A little sleep, a little slumber, a little folding
of the hands to rest"—**

**Your poverty will come in like a vagabond and
your need like an armed man (Proverbs 6:6-11).**

A sluggard, to whom Solomon is referring in these
verses, is basically a lazy person. Ants are always
working, focused, devoted, and preparing for the future.
As we learn to rise above the temptation to rest too
much, we will become more diligent. Thomas Edison said
this well: "If I were a school teacher, I would put lazy
pupils to studying bees and ants. They would soon learn
to be diligent."

When there is a goal to be accomplished, many plea-
sures may have to be set aside for a time. This may
include watching television, going to movies, even visiting
with friends—the very things we may love to do in our

leisure time. Most people have a day job, so the only available time to work toward goals not associated with work are in the evening or on weekends. Something must be sacrificed. Amazingly though, it will not seem so much like work, especially when the goal is completed. Robert Schuller said: "Most people who succeed in the face of seemingly impossible conditions are people who simply don't know how to quit." We must not quit until the goal is accomplished. And when it is, there is nothing sweeter than seeing that work completed.

Edison actually thrived and enjoyed his work, staying focused throughout his life. He said: "I never did a day's work in my life. It was all fun." I truly believe that—when we are doing what we have been born to do, it does become fun. God gives us special gifts in that area to make it easier. We just have to find what we do best and do it. Edison should give us great hope that we can follow through with the power of focus to finish what the Lord has given us to do. His life was rich with accomplishments. Ours can be as well.

Opportunity is missed by most people because
it is dressed in overalls and looks like work.
Genius is one percent inspiration and
ninety-nine percent perspiration.
~Thomas Edison

CHAPTER SIX

THE POWER OF OVERCOMING

CHARLES M. SCHULZ, AN OVERCOMER

If I were given the opportunity to present a gift to the next generation, it would be the ability for each individual to learn to laugh at himself.
~ Charles Schulz

Charles M. Schulz was an overcomer. His past did not hinder his future—it actually propelled him into his lifelong profession as a cartoonist. As we reflect upon his life, we will see how he overcame what may seem to have been shortcomings to launch himself into a victorious life.

The famous comic strip, *Peanuts*, written by Charles Schulz, was published for fifty years. He won the hearts of millions of people with characters to whom everyone could relate. Who could forget Charlie Brown? He was a loser who never won a baseball game, nor was he ever able to kick a football. He was always attempting to triumph over adversity.

Sometimes I lie awake at night, and I ask, "Where have I gone wrong?" Then a voice says to me, "This is going to take more than one night."

~Charles M. Schulz, (Charlie Brown)

How about Snoopy, Charlie Brown's dog, Schulz' most popular creation? He imagined himself as a World War I flying ace right on his doghouse, and he was always dancing and smiling. What about Linus and his security blanket? And Lucy who for a nickel gave counseling sessions out of her psychiatrist's booth? When Snoopy kissed her, Lucy hysterically said, "Auugh! I've been kissed by a dog! I have dog germs! Get some hot water! Get some disinfectant! Get some iodine!" And we laugh at the nonsense of the moment. All Schulz' characters had their own unique personalities, endearing them to us.

Yesterday I was a dog. Today I'm a dog. Tomorrow I'll probably still be a dog. Sigh! There's so little hope for advancement.

~Charles M. Schulz (Snoopy)

SPARKY

Charles Monroe Schulz was born on November 26, 1922 to Dena and Carl Schulz, neither of whom were educated beyond third grade. His closest friends and family called him "Sparky," a nickname after Sparkplug, the horse in the comic strip *Barney Google*. Schulz led an ordinary life as a child—his father was a barber and his mother a homemaker. He felt deep insecurities as a child; he knew that his mom and dad loved him but he just was not convinced other people would ever care as much.

Schulz was intelligent in school—skipping ahead twice by half-grades in third and fifth. He was lonely and unsure of himself, being the youngest and smallest in his classes. So, perhaps this added to the feeling as a teenager that he felt invisible at times. Yet, at the same time he was growing increasingly independent.

He felt "no one ever gave him credit for his drawing, or for playing a superior game of golf."[1] But there was one who recognized his talent—his mother. His family did not have much extra money, and the cost for a drawing course was $170—a huge undertaking financially. Still, she sent off for a correspondence course in art for Schulz, which proved an excellent investment.

Painfully, at age twenty, his mother died, and he was drafted into the army within three days of her death. Soon thereafter he was on his way to Camp Campbell, Kentucky as a private. He survived World War II while serving in Europe and left the army as a sergeant. But when he returned home, he seemed lost, not really feeling much hope for the future—his beloved mother was gone and he felt a deep sense of loss.

TIMELESS TOPIX

But gradually he snapped out of the depression that seemed to plague him. He took a job lettering comic strips for *Timeless Topix,* a Catholic-oriented comic magazine. "*Timeless Topix* eventually became the first publisher of Schulz's cartoons. Two issues of the magazine featured Schulz doing pages of cartoons about little kids, a topic he discovered he liked."[2]

While Schulz was in his lettering career, he took an instructor's job at the same correspondence school from which he had studied as a youth. "This proved a vital place for his personal growth. During his time at the school, Schulz fell in love with (and was ultimately rejected by) his own little red-haired girl. He was also encouraged by a co-worker to submit some of his cartoons to a local paper."[3]

LI'L FOLKS

His cartoon entitled *Li'l Folks* debuted on December 7, 1947, in the *St. Paul Pioneer Press.* He also sold similar cartoons to magazines, such as *The Saturday Evening Post.* It took courage and boldness for Schulz to even attempt to sell his cartoons. But when opportunity knocks, as he learned, we must go for it. As Alexander Graham Bell once said: "Sometimes we stare so long at a door that is closing that we see too late the one that is open." We must learn to seize an opportunity when it arises. Schulz could see an opportunity open before him and he went for it. Timing can be everything. *The Saturday Evening Post* bought seventeen of his cartoons and they were published between 1948 and 1950, giving his cartoons national exposure.

PEANUTS

His biggest break came in June of 1950, when *Li'l Folks* aroused the interest of Jim Freeman at United Features Syndicate. They renamed the cartoon *Peanuts.* Schulz felt the name seemed like it was unimportant. Even so, it debuted as *Peanuts* on October 2, 1950 in seven papers and *Peanuts* rapidly grew in popularity. *The Washington Post,* which was one of the seven papers that originally carried the strip, ran it until the end. At its peak, "it was syndicated to more than 2,600 newspapers around the world, appeared in about 25 languages, and reached an estimated audience of 355 million."[4] "Schulz became the most highly paid, most widely read cartoonist ever...earning from $30 to $40 million a year."[5]

When Schulz gave life to Charlie Brown (who was named after a friend from art school) in his syndicated cartoon, it would in many ways be a reflection of himself, which is why his character was so believable. He was real. Charlie Brown's father was a barber, just like Schulz' father. Had it not been for his trials and problems as a child, he might never had had the depth of feeling to create such a character as Charlie Brown. Schulz also had a dog named Spike, but he was a pointer, rather than a beagle like Snoopy. Schulz was also rejected by a red-haired girl, just like Charlie Brown. He drew so much from his life experiences that he could write from his heart.

David Michaelis said this about Schulz and his cartoon *Peanuts*:

> This was something new in the newspaper comic strip...Schulz dared to use his own quirks—a lifelong sense of alienation, insecurity, and inferiority—to draw the real feelings of his life and time. He brought a spare pen line, Jack Benny timing, and a subtle sense of humor to taboo themes such as faith, intolerance, depression, loneliness, cruelty, and despair. His characters were contemplative. They spoke with simplicity and force. They made smart observations about literature, art, classical music, theology, medicine, psychiatry, sports, and the law.[6]

As a side note on Schulz' personal life, in 1951 he married Joyce Halverson. They eventually had five children, but later divorced. He married his second wife, Jean Forsyth Clyde in 1973, and stayed married to her the remainder of his life. He had a strong sense of family, and derived some of his material from events with his own children. He was able to draw from his own life circumstances and share this with others. Is this not the way it is in our own lives? We are able to give from the life we live.

A CHARLIE BROWN CHRISTMAS

On December 5, 1965, *A Charlie Brown Christmas* aired. Network executives were concerned and predicted "that its cartoon format, melancholy jazz score by Vincent Guaraldi and simple retelling of the Nativity story from the Gospel of Luke would alienate the public."[7] However, *A Charlie Brown Christmas* was a great success, winning Emmy and Peabody awards. To this day it is a Christmas-time tradition. This first exposure of *Peanuts* led to many more animated television specials, a television series, and even four feature films. Thus began the amazing popularity of the *Peanuts* cartoon. "An entire industry of *Peanuts* related merchandise swept the nation. Everything from jewelry to lunch boxes, as well as dolls, clothing and greeting cards featured the gang. Snoopy even became something of a corporate spokesman. One result of all this was an income for Schulz estimated at $33 million by *Forbes* magazine in 1995 and 1996."[8]

A MAN OF GOD

Charles M. Schulz loved God. He was a member and Sunday School teacher at the Church of God. "Biblical themes and references were a common feature of Peanuts throughout its fifty-year run; by one estimate, 10 percent of the 18,000 strips involved religion."[9]

Schulz also drew the cartoons for Robert Short's 1965 best-seller (more than 10 million copies sold) *The Gospel According to Peanuts*, which was about Christian parables. Schulz once told *Decision* magazine: "Humor which does not say anything is worthless humor...so I contend that a cartoonist must be given a chance to do his own preaching."

Schulz made this statement about how he felt about God.

> *...The more I thought about the matter during those Bible studies the more I realized that I really loved God...I cannot point to a specific time of dedication to Christ; I was just suddenly 'there,' and did not know when it happened that I arrived. I feel a constant gratefulness to God for His patience with me and with all of us. I cannot fail to be thrilled every time I read the things that Jesus said, and I am more and more convinced of the necessity of following Him. What Jesus means to me is this: In Him we are able to see God and to understand His feelings toward us.*

Schulz believed that when we accept Jesus, our problems are not automatically solved. Sometimes there are battles—real ones to face. His characters faced plenty of problems, but we learned to laugh with them even in the face of defeat—especially in the case of Charlie Brown. But we loved him for it.

One cartoon featured Charlie Brown pitching a baseball and saying, "Thou shalt not be afraid of the terror by night, nor of the pestilence that walketh in darkness." Then a ball whizzes by, knocking him down. The final frame features Charlie Brown following up the words from Psalm 91: "But those line drives will kill you!"[10]

HEALING WITH HUMOR

Schulz worked alone for three decades, and he felt if he could draw his four panels a day, all would be well in his life. Schulz believed that through humor we can heal many wounds in our lives, even those from childhood. Schulz allowed us to see the funnier side of life with the *Peanuts* gang. Humor relieves the seriousness in life. Hard times will come, but perhaps if we can find some humor during those times, we too will begin to laugh at ourselves, finding that it relieves stress.

Don't worry about the world coming to an end today. It's already tomorrow in Australia.

~Charles M. Schulz

In one of Schulz' cartoons, Charlie Brown puts forth his best, positive thinking as he tries to stop Lucy from hitting the ball: He's thinking, "If you throw a fast ball right across the center of the plate...." But as usual, it does not work, and Lucy hits the ball out of the park. As the balls flies by him, he is swept off his feet. And we laugh. Schulz wants us to see the comedy of life. He wants us to know that Charlie Brown will try once again to get things right. And we shall do so as well.

Schulz was the most successful cartoonists ever. Why? He could draw cartoons that touched the hearts of everyone. We could all relate to how Charlie Brown and the rest of the gang felt. He made us see that even though life has its struggles, we can still find humor in many situations, if we look. He knew exactly how Charlie Brown felt because he was Charlie Brown in many ways. Schulz was an overcomer. He left the past behind, yet was able to relate his trials and triumphs through a bunch of kids. He preached through his cartoons, yet we did not really know it.

He did not draw cartoons about war and hard times—news and life took care of those things. We could daily read his cartoon and just laugh sometimes at the absurdity of life. He made life lighter and happier for many people, and that in itself is a great triumph. Two Scriptures in Proverbs explain the benefits of being happy: **"A merry heart does good, like medicine..." (Proverbs 17:22 NKJV)** and **"A merry heart makes a cheerful countenance..." (Proverbs 15:13 NKJV).**

Schulz was a hard worker, daily working in his studio alone. He always pictured himself drawing until he was in his eighties. But his life took a different turn in November of 1999 when he had a stroke, and later doctors discovered he had colon cancer. The stroke and surgery robbed Schulz of his will to keep drawing. He struggled to see clearly and could not recall the words that he needed. On December 14, 1999, at age seventy-seven, he announced his retirement. On February 12, 2000, Charles M. Schulz died peacefully, just hours before the final *Peanuts* strip appeared in Sunday newspapers around the world.

His legacy of cartoon characters will live on forever through books and animated cartoons written by this special man. May we all learn from Charles M. Schulz that we too can overcome our past, knowing that God allowed those things to happen for a reason. What we learn from our hardships of the past will actually propel us into who we are, enabling us to help others in those same areas as well. May we also learn to look at life a little lighter, laughing at ourselves, rather than pounding ourselves for our mistakes. Yes, we all have made mistakes, but it is what we choose to do with those mistakes that will dictate our future. We can think about them daily or learn from them and go on, being set free to help others. Choosing to overcome is a powerful choice. Charles M. Schulz was an overcomer, an awesome man who enabled many people to laugh daily—and he still does—what a legacy.

All you need is love. But a little chocolate now and then doesn't hurt.

~ Charles M. Schulz

◆ ◆ ◆ ◆ ◆

CONCLUSION

A life filled with purpose has power. This power enabled the six remarkable people that we studied to fulfill what they were born to do. Each overcame adversity throughout their lives and had passion for their purpose, vision, devotion, perseverance, and focus. They also left a legacy behind—something to benefit others.

The power-filled fire, which burned steadily within them to accomplish so much in their lives, can be ignited in us as well. By learning from the lessons that were illuminated by these six, we, too, can experience the power of fulfilling our own purpose in life.

When it is time for us to leave this earth, we all want to have successfully completed the course that the Lord gave us to do from the beginning. The challenge is before us. May we learn from these extraordinary people to go beyond what we think we can do and fulfill our destiny. Jesus said, **"...with God all things are possible" (Matthew 19:26).** With faith, we can follow our pathway to purpose and finish!

Faith makes all things possible...
love makes all things easy.
~Dwight L. Moody

CHAPTER SEVEN

OVERCOMING FEAR

Courage is contagious.
When a brave man takes a stand,
the spines of others are often stiffened.
~Billy Graham

HINDRANCES

Many hindrances can stop us from walking forward in our purpose in life. Once these obstacles are brought to the light, recognized, and conquered, we can fulfill all that we have been called to do. In this chapter and the following four, we will discuss fear, procrastination, impatience, discouragement, and guilt—five of the main hindrances that we must conquer if we are ever to fulfill our destinies.

OVERCOMING FEAR

One area that can hinder us from fulfilling our purpose in life is fear. Fear is like a vice that grips and smothers the faith that seeks to arise from within. If we allow fear to overtake us, then it will stop us in completing any goal.

When we face difficult tasks, anxiety is the enemy that will try to operate and steal the victory. Anxiety is rooted in fear. By casting our anxiety upon the Lord, we are trusting Him to help us. Then we will be filled with His peace, which abolishes all fear. **"The steadfast of mind Thou wilt keep in perfect peace, because he trusts in Thee (Isaiah 26:3).** The Lord tells us to cast all of our anxiety upon Him because He loves and cares for us (see I Peter 5:7). His desire is for us to overcome and not succumb to fear.

By continually turning to the Lord and trusting that He will deliver us from fear, we will begin to see this stronghold leave our lives. I John 4:18 states: **"There is no fear in love [dread does not exist] but full-grown (complete, perfect) love turns fear out of doors and expels every trace of terror!..."**(AMP) The Lord loves us so much that He wants fear to be expelled from our lives! As we grasp the concept of His love, His peace will rule in our hearts, we will grow in our trust of the Lord, and become more focused on Him, thus enabling us to press on toward fulfilling our callings.

Many people have a fear of speaking in front of an audience. When asked to speak or to do something that may cause us to have fear, we must face it, and do it in faith. By having faith in God, which is complete trust in Him, He will give us peace and confidence to fulfill any task. Fear cannot abide with faith. As we boldly face the fear that hinders us in faith, fear will lose its grip and no longer have power over us. Eleanor Roosevelt made this comment about fear: "I believe that anyone can conquer fear by doing the things he fears to do...."

When we truly know the Lord, then we know that His love will cast out all fear. Jesus says in John 14:27: **"Peace I leave with you; My peace I give to you; not as the world gives, do I give to you. Let not your heart be troubled, nor let it be fearful."** When we become filled with fear, we should acknowledge in faith that the Lord is with us, and believe that He will consume the fear for He is the **"Prince of Peace"** (see Isaiah 9:6).

Courage comes when we take action in the midst of fear, and courage will overthrow fear every time. In the Bible one shining example of someone who overcame fear with courage was Esther.

FOR SUCH A TIME AS THIS

Esther knew that any man or woman who had not been called to go into the inner court of the king would be put to death, unless the king held out his golden scepter. Esther had not been called before King Ahasuerus in thirty days, but she knew she had to talk to him about an urgent matter. The life of her people, the Jews, depended upon her. She had a choice to make—she could surrender to fear or courageously go before the king and fulfill her destiny. Mordecai knew that God was going to deliver the Jews, but he also knew that God had chosen Esther to deliver them. We, too, will have choices to make. We can let fear control us or boldly walk forward in faith and do what we have been called to do. We have also been called **"for such a time as this." (Esther 4:14 NKJV).**

Esther was so convinced that she must go before the king in an effort to save her people that she was even willing to lay down her life. How many of us are so committed to the Lord and the call He has placed on our lives that we are willing to die for Him? The Lord is calling the courageous, those with resolute steadfastness who will come before His throne and answer His call. Ecclesiastes 9:10 states: **"whatever your hand finds to do, verily, do it with all your might...."** Being valiant with unwavering faith will enable us to finish the specific tasks we have been called to accomplish.

So it was with Esther. After three days, she put on her royal robes and courageously went before the king. She waited to see if the king would receive her. Indeed he did. When King Ahasuerus saw her, she found favor in his eyes and he held out his golden scepter. She was now in position to fulfill her destiny. Because of her boldness, she was able stop the enemy's plans of destroying her people. Haman, the king's wicked advisor, was exposed and his plan of destroying the Jews was stopped because of her decisive actions. Instead of the Jews being destroyed, the king allowed them to destroy their enemies!

CONFRONT FEARS

God will shine His favor upon us as we follow His will for our lives. We should never fear anything He has called us to do. If He has given us a task to do, there will always be a way. As we boldly step forward to fulfill our callings, God will be with us. It is clear from Hebrews 10:38 that God is not pleased when we surrender to fear.

"But the just shall live by faith [My righteous servant shall live by his conviction respecting man's relationship to God and divine things, and holy fervor born of faith and conjoined with it]; and if he draws back and shrinks in fear, My soul has no delight or pleasure in him (AMP).

As fears are confronted and we walk in faith, God will be pleased. He is readily available to help in any situation—we just need to ask. **"On the day I called Thou didst answer me; Thou didst make me bold with strength in my soul" (Psalm 138:3).** He will give us boldness and strength in any circumstance. He will honor our faith in Him, and help us achieve His desire for our lives.

DAVID, A MAN OF FAITH

David had tremendous faith in God, and he had no doubt that the Lord would deliver him in any situation. The Lord had proven faithful by giving him the skill to kill both lions and bears.

To David, a man who taunted the armies of the living God was not tolerable. He was angered by Goliath's ridicule of God and he could no longer allow Goliath to continue doing this.

Goliath stood more than nine feet tall and was a champion among the Philistines. He was clothed from head to foot in bronze armor, a menacing sight to behold. Nobody wanted to fight him because of his size and bully attitude. I have often wondered what David thought when he first saw Goliath. Fear could have easily taken his faith, but he did not allow it. God had delivered him before and He would again. There was simply no doubt in his mind that God was with him, so David put his plan into action. He knew he had to bring this giant down. He wore no armor and took a sling and five stones from the brook as his only weapons. This is what David said to Goliath:

> **"You come to me with a sword, a spear, and a javelin, but I come to you in the name of the LORD of hosts, the God of the armies of Israel, whom you have taunted.**
>
> **This day the LORD will deliver you up into my hands, and I will strike you down and remove your head from you. And I will give the dead bodies of the army of the Philistines this day to the birds of the sky and the wild beasts of the earth, that all the earth may know that there is a God in Israel,**
>
> **and that all this assembly may know that the LORD does not deliver by sword or by spear; for the battle is the LORD's and He will give you into our hands" (I Samuel 17:45-47).**

Imagine how angry this made Goliath! David was now facing a giant, who was even more angered than he had been five minutes ago because of what David had just said to him. David knew he had little time. He acted upon faith and ran toward Goliath, pulled out a stone, and slung it at him. It sank into the forehead of Goliath with such force that he died instantly. David never doubted that God would deliver Goliath into his hands. The above prophecy proved true and David became a hero.

David had no doubt that God would indeed be the Deliverer. Having faith always means taking action. As we walk forward in faith, it will override fear every time and God will bless us because we believe in faith that no matter what comes our way, He will be our Deliverer!

Fear cannot abide with faith, for they have nothing in common. We cannot progress forward in what we have been called to do if fear rules our hearts. As our relationship with the Lord grows, we will begin to have a deeper trust in Him. We will come to the place where we believe we can do anything.

The work ahead may be difficult, but a closer relationship with the Lord will be the reward. When we have fulfilled our callings, there will be satisfaction in knowing we have pleased the Lord by completing the course He has ordained for our lives. May we all learn from Esther and David that no task is too great. Both were brave and did indeed fulfill their destinies. In faith, we can do the same.

Don't waste life in doubts and fears;
spend yourself on the work before you,
well assured that the right performance of
this hour's duties will be the best preparation
for the hours and ages that will follow it.
~ Ralph Waldo Emerson

CHAPTER EIGHT

PREVAILING OVER PROCRASTINATION

It's a job that's never started
that takes the longest to finish.
~J. R. R. Tolkien

Another area that will stop us from achieving our purpose in life is procrastination, which is habitually postponing something that could be done today. All truth is ageless, as this famous quote by Benjamin Franklin still proves true today: "Never leave that till tomorrow which you can do today." When we continually say we will do something tomorrow, it will never get done. Edward Young, a seventeenth century English poet, said this well: "Procrastination is the thief of time."

A person who procrastinates will shift his attention from a great idea to eventually making an excuse to not do it, which is basically not putting the idea into action. A procrastinator will begin many projects, but never finish any of them, leaving him or her frustrated. Procrastinators see all the problems about reaching their goal, rather than the promise of success. Thomas Edison once said: "The value of an idea lies in the using of it." In other words, many people have great ideas, but they are of no value if they are not brought to fruition. The important thing is to finish.

A negative side effect of procrastination is added stress to our lives. In life, we will we have many deadlines. The procrastinator will put off that which seems difficult to the very last minute—things like preparing tax returns, paying bills, Christmas shopping, house repairs, studying for an exam, or working on a project that is due the next day—do any of those sound familiar? When we wait to do anything at the last minute, we will not do our best because a time element is now added to finishing the goal. Time can be a friend, but it can also be an enemy if we wait until the last minute to accomplish what we know we must do.

MAKE A PLAN

One suggestion to help in the area of procrastination is to write in a notebook what needs to be accomplished that day. Make an actual schedule if you have a tendency to waste time, and devise a plan. Even if you have to begin by writing down what you will do every hour, start there. It will give you a great sense of accomplishment, enabling you to feel that you can complete something of worth as you check off each goal as it is fulfilled. As you progress in finishing these smaller goals and feel comfortable that you can reach them without writing down an hourly schedule, then plan what you will do for the day. Always check off goals as they are finished. As you see yourself completing specific goals, you will accomplish more and more. Once you have the momentum built in reaching a goal, do not stop until you finish it, remembering that on the other side of procrastination is the sweet victory of success.

You will also want to write down your large goals for life and put them in a place where you will see them daily. It may take years to accomplish even one goal, but as you accomplish one—check it off. As you use this plan of daily working toward completing a goal, you will eventually accomplish those larger goals. What a great feeling it is to complete something of worth.

Have you ever noticed how time vanishes? We cannot take back a second of the past, but we can learn to use our present and future time wisely. There are many ways to do this. The best way I have discovered is to maintain my focus and push through until I finish my goal.

Two important skills that we must develop in order to conquer procrastination are discipline and determination. These skills will help us to stay focused and finish the task. By using these strategically, procrastination will be defeated.

DISCIPLINE

As one of my callings in life is to write, I will apply what I have learned about discipline to writing, but these can be applied to any purpose.

It takes discipline to finally finish a writing project. Sometimes I get writer's block, which is like a wall that blocks my thoughts. I find that if I can write daily, it will flow much easier when I need to write an article or continue with a larger project. It is extremely important to discipline yourself to work daily on your project, your goal, and gradually the work will get finished. Some days you may just have fifteen minutes to work, but that is fifteen minutes of new work on the project. Steady progress is the key. Remember, if you never start, you will never finish.

If we will be faithful to work on our goals, the Lord will be faithful to help us. We have the best Helper of all living inside of us—the Holy Spirit. We can accomplish any goal the Lord has given to us. He was the One who gave it to us to do. Therefore, He knows we have the skills to accomplish it. Henry Ford once said: "Whether you think you can, or whether you think you can't—you are right!" If you will set your eyes toward your goal and not lose focus, determining to never quit, you will finish it.

Let's say you have determined it is God's will for you to write a book. That is wonderful! But may I make a suggestion? Begin by writing an article. It is not such a vast project and it will be far easier to accomplish than writing a book. Once you have success with writing an article, keep writing more and more. Eventually, you will write the book that is your heart's desire. Success is the satisfaction of completing what you set out to do. Start working toward accomplishing smaller goals. Then after these are achieved, work toward the larger goals. The more you accomplish, the more you will want to accomplish.

DISCIPLINE DEFEATS DISTRACTIONS

The enemy is a master of deception, and procrastination is an easy ploy he sends to many because he knows the battle is hard to win. Distractions in abundance will come, if we allow them. It is quite easy to fall into the trap of being distracted. Say you have determined to begin working on a project and you walk by the television and your favorite show is on. There are two choices— one, watch the show or two, walk past it and work on the project. Of course, we know the best choice is to walk past it and begin working on the project. By remaining focused on your goal, distractions will not steal your time. It takes discipline to say "no" when temptation comes. Walk away from the temptation and the victory is won. And, when you begin working on the project, there is a triumph that adds inspiration to the project.

There is no easy way to become a good writer without plenty of practice. Writing is hard work and it may take hours, days, weeks, or even years of research before the writing actually begins. To become an excellent writer, it takes discipline and hard work, which is something we must embrace in any project. The best way to become a good writer or get better at any skill is to practice daily. C. S. Lewis once said: "A professional writer is an amateur who didn't quit." In any new field we are all beginners; it is those who keep working who become the professionals.

If you are faithful to begin a goal, the Lord will help you finish it. Remember what the Lord said, **"He who is faithful in a very little thing is faithful also in much; and he who is unrighteous in a very little thing is unrighteous also in much (Luke 16:10).**

Use the talents faithfully that the Lord has given you, and He will give you more.

> Even if you are on the right track,
> you'll get run over if you just sit there.
> ~Will Rogers

CHAPTER NINE

OVERCOMING IMPATIENCE

God is never in a hurry.
~ Oswald Chambers

In a world that has every convenience at its fingertips, the word "patience" will have a negative connotation to most. We have become a fast-paced society with computer technology, video games, television, and movies, which have become so dramatic that "edge of the seat" experiences happen one after another. We have fast food restaurants with very little waiting and microwave dinners that may be heated and eaten in a matter of minutes. Flying across the country takes a matter of hours, and within seconds we can be on the phone with someone in another country. These conveniences may be helpful, but they may also be detrimental if we expect everything to come to us this quickly.

If we are impatient, we will have a tendency to be self-centered and lead stressful lives. Peace will not be part of our lives because we are in too much of a hurry to embrace "rest." There is a restlessness associated with impatient people and it will actually stop the flow of creativity. If we are impatient, our work usually amounts to little or nothing because of the tendency to finish the project too quickly. Work that is hurried is only mediocre at best.

When we become impatient, frustration may cause us to take matters into our own hands. We may fulfill a fleshly desire, but this impatience will cause us to miss God's best. Remember the story of Ishmael? Because of impatience and unbelief, Sarah gave Hagar, her maid, to Abraham as a wife so she could have a child through her. As God had already promised Abraham that he would have a child by Sarah, Abraham displayed unbelief by not waiting to have a child by her. As soon as the child was conceived through Hagar, Sarah knew that her scheme had been wrong, but there was no turning back. Hagar's son was Ishmael, and from his lineage came the religion of Islam, a distortion and great enemy of Israel and Christianity.

PATIENCE, A VIRTUE

Patience must be a virtue within us if we are ever to accomplish anything of worth in this life. Most accomplishments do not come easily, so we must know from the beginning that it will take work, perseverance, and patience to accomplish goals.

James explains to us the great benefits of being patient:

> **My brethren, count it all joy when you fall into various trials,**

knowing that the testing of your faith produces patience.

But let patience have its perfect work, that you may *be perfect and complete, lacking nothing* (emphasis mine, **James 1:2-4 NKJV**).

According to James, we should be happy when we encounter trials because **"the testing of your faith produces patience."** First, let us think about the word **"testing."** When I looked up this word in the *Webster's Dictionary*, I was amazed at one of the meanings—"an event, set of circumstances, etc. that proves or tries a person's qualities." Faith should actually be a quality in our character. When it is tested and proven, and we do indeed have faith, then patience will grow within us. So we can conclude from this Scripture that there is a correlation between faith and patience—the more faith we have in our lives, the more patient we will be.

According to Hebrews 6:12, it takes faith and patience to inherit the promises. But to have both we must allow faith to produce patience within us. When we have faith, we do not need evidence to believe—we just know that whatever we believe will happen, no matter how long it takes. This indeed is patience. When we are patient, we do not complain but endure the waiting. Lamentations 3:25 states: **"The LORD is good to those who wait for Him, to the person who seeks Him."**

The Israelites wandered in the desert for forty years because of their murmuring and complaining, which was basically rooted in impatience. Let us learn now to remove complaining from our lives. When we complain, we are decreasing the faith within us, which will in turn decrease our patience.

"**But let patience have its perfect work, that you may be perfect and complete, lacking nothing**" **(James 1:4** NKJV**)** Now we come to the benefits of being patient. If we can allow patience to be worked into our lives, we can actually be **"perfect and complete, lacking nothing."** You may ask: How can we be perfect and complete just by being patient? The Lord knows how difficult it is to be patient, and if we can be perfected in this one area, then most likely we will also have the other fruits of the Spirit in our life as well. The fruits of the Spirit are: **"love, joy, peace, patience, kindness, goodness, faithfulness, gentleness, self-control..."** **(Galatians 5:22-23).** As we allow the Lord to work more deeply in our lives, these character traits should be who we really are. Paul explains to us in I Corinthians 13:4 that **"Love is patient"** so we can conclude that to be patient is to love. If we are kind, we are patient. If we have goodness, we are patient. If we have faithfulness, we are patient, and so on. Now, we can see that to be patient is to be **"perfect and complete, lacking nothing."**

In my allegorical book, *The Chosen Path,* Zoe has been invited on a journey to Remiah, where the King lives. Along her adventurous journey, she must acquire nine keys, which are named after each fruit of the Spirit. Each time she earns a key, she is changed, becoming more like the King every day. To reach Remiah, she must acquire all the keys, and some were extremely difficult to receive. Likewise, the road to Him will be hard at times, but in the end it will all be worth it, because we are being changed into His image so we can be with Him. The Lord wants His bride spotless, not tainted with sin. Just as Zoe had the adventure of her life while being changed into the King's image, so can we! The purpose in life that the Lord gives each of us is the very thing we have always wanted to do. Even so, it will take patience to finish our courses.

If we can become patient and persevere through whatever circumstances may occur in our lives, we will complete that which we have been called to do. It is our faith that will produce the patience to finish. We have learned that to have vision is to actually see (through faith) the end result of our goal *before* it happens. Faith and patience are connected.

As we work toward accomplishing individual goals, which will ultimately achieve the complete purpose to which we have been called, let us do it as unto the Lord so it will please Him. As we do our work for Him, we will want to do our very best. Many times we will need to sit quietly (with patience!) and wait before the Lord, and then He will give us instruction. Quality time spent with Him is never wasted. His inspiration is freely given if we will seek Him. Not only will we receive from Him, but our relationships will grow with Him. And after all, our time spent with Him is by far the most important time we will ever spend in our lives. Fulfilling our purpose in life should be an outgrowth of the special time we spend with Him.

We should all be accomplishing great things because we have His creativity flowing through us, but doing works will never be as important as being with the Lord. **"Whatever you do, do your work heartily, as for the Lord rather than for men, knowing that from the Lord you will receive the reward of the inheritance..." (Colossians 3:23-24).**

With faith and patience, you can accomplish your purpose. Do not lose sight of the One who will instruct you with His patience. He is the Guide to finishing that which He has called you to do.

Everything comes to him that
hustles while he waits.
~ Thomas Edison

CHAPTER TEN

DEFEATING DISCOURAGEMENT

Many of life's failures are people who
did not realize how close they were
to success when they gave up.
~ Thomas Edison

W hen we become discouraged, it is a struggle to do much of anything, especially to fulfill a goal. *Webster's Dictionary* defines discouragement like this: "to deprive of courage, hope, or confidence; dishearten." Discouragement is the absence of courage. Without courage, we will not have the boldness to tackle even the smallest goal in life.

Discouragement is truly an enemy and we must fight it at every turn. Discouragement cost one generation of Israelites a blessed life in the Promised Land. When God delivered them from the Egyptians, who had enslaved them for generations, He intended for them to live a good life. Moses sent twelve men, one from each tribe, to go and spy out the Promised Land. They were pleased with the land and **"they also took some of the fruit of** the land in their hands and brought it down to us; and they brought back word to us, saying, 'It is a good land which the LORD our God is giving us'" (Deuteronomy 1:25 NKJV). The fruit was huge and scrumptious and the land was theirs for the taking.

But fear took their hearts when they saw the size of the men they would have to fight to attain the Promised Land; then they became discouraged. Moses was not happy with them when he heard their complaining and fear. He told them: **"and you complained in your tents, and said, 'Because the LORD hates us, He has brought us out of the land of Egypt to deliver us into the hand of the Amorites, to destroy us. Where can we go up? Our brethren have *discouraged* our hearts, saying, 'The people are greater and taller than we; the cities are great and fortified up to heaven; moreover we have seen the sons of the Anakim there'"** (emphasis mine, **Deuteronomy 1:27-28 NKJV**).

They became so discouraged and depressed that they were deceived into believing that the Lord hated them! Yet, He had delivered them from a horrible life in Egypt, as Moses reminded them. And, had they just had faith, He would have helped them fight the Amorites and win the battle. Moses tried to help them see the truth: **"Do not be terrified, or afraid of them. The LORD your God, who goes before you, He will fight for you, according to all He did for you in Egypt before your eyes, and in the wilderness where you saw how the LORD your God carried you, as a man carries his son, in all the way that you went until you came to this place. Yet, for all that, you did not believe the LORD your God (Deuteronomy 1:29-32 NKJV).**

Because they allowed discouragement to grip them, they did not feel they could win the battle and they even turned on the Lord!

God became very angry with His chosen people. **"And the LORD heard the sound of your words, and was angry, and took an oath, saying, 'Surely not one of these men of this evil generation shall see that good land of which I swore to give to your fathers, except Caleb the son of Jephunneh; he shall see it, and to him and his children I am giving the land on which he walked, because he wholly followed the LORD...Joshua the son of Nun, who stands before you he shall go in there." (Deuteronomy 1:34-36, 38 NKJV).** Joshua and Caleb believed that they could take the land easily, but the Israelites would not listen, until it was too late. Only Caleb and Joshua were able to go to the Promised Land. A whole generation lost out on the blessing of a wonderful life because they believed the discouraging report from men, rather than to fight and take the land that the Lord had promised them.

FIGHT DISCOURAGEMENT

Satan does not want any of us to live the kind of life we were born to live. We cannot and must not listen to his lies. When we become discouraged, we must fight the battle he has set against us until we win. And just like the Lord would have helped the Israelites, the Lord will help us win the battle. Discouragement can be devastating in our lives. We must not let it rule!

We have all faced discouragement, but we must fight this ongoing enemy if we are to ever succeed in fulfilling our purpose in life. Discouragement can drain the life out of us until it is a struggle to focus on anything. Galatians 6:9 gives us courage to keep going: **"So don't get tired of doing what is good. Don't get discouraged and give up, for we will reap a harvest of blessing at the appropriate time"** (NLT).

The enemy would enjoy seeing us discouraged all the time—this, however, is not God's plan for us! We may all be familiar with the Scripture in Philippians 4:13, but do we truly believe it? **"I can do all things through Him who strengthens me."** The Lord is the One who gives us the strength to do what He has called us to do. We must never lose sight of this.

When we become discouraged, the Lord is only a prayer away, and He will help us. Just as Psalm 27:14 says: **"Wait for the LORD; be strong, and let your heart take courage; yes, wait for the LORD."** God is with us. We must have the faith to believe this. He does not want to see us discouraged in any way, for it is a sad and lonely place to be. We can triumph in the area of discouragement through faith, believing that God is for us.

Do not ever give up on your dreams. Discouragement will drain your creativity and make you think it is not worth the cost. Take courage and fight for your dreams with all your might. Every battle will be worth it in the end. Norman Vincent Peal said this well: "Stand up to your obstacles and do something about them. You will find that they haven't half the strength you think they have."

Remember Jim Valvano's famous line:

"Don't give up; don't ever give up!"

PLOW THROUGH

Like many, I have had to fight discouragement much of my life and I have learned many lessons in my battles. A huge lesson I have learned is to take authority over my thoughts. Let me explain. A series of events happened during one week and I was feeling discouraged; I just could not shake it. It became worse as the week progressed. Discouragement was choking the very life out of me. I knew I needed to overcome, but I could not seem to do it.

On Friday evening of that week I was working in my garden, and as I began to remove the weeds with a hoe, the thought occurred to me to plow through how I was feeling. I wondered how to do this and then I realized I should begin thanking the Lord for all of the blessings in my life. Even though I did not feel like it, I began praising Him, and before long, I found that my eyes were no longer focused on myself, but were focused on Him. As I continued to praise Him for His goodness, discouragement began to dissipate and I actually began to feel happy again. I had plowed through discouragement and had sown the exact opposite of what I was feeling. The Lord gave me the reward of joy. Hebrews 13:15 exhorts us to **"… continually offer up a sacrifice of praise to God, that is, the fruit of lips that give thanks to His name."** By offering praise to the Lord, truly thanking Him for all He has done in our lives, we will find that discouragement will not have a grip on us and it will actually leave.

You only have the time the Lord has given to you. What will you do with your time? What is it that burns within you to accomplish? Do not let the fire go out until your goals are reached! You will never be truly happy until you are doing what you were born to do. Helen Keller once said: "Many people have a wrong idea of what constitutes true happiness. It is not attained through self-gratification, but through fidelity to a worthy purpose." Coming from a woman who was deaf and blind, this statement has amazing meaning. She accomplished far more goals in her life than most do with all their five senses. Helen Keller learned the key to this happiness is to begin, and then to finish something that is of worth. Remember, however, you cannot finish what you do not start.

Take the first step in faith.
You don't have to see the whole
staircase, just take the first step.
~ Dr. Martin Luther King Jr.

CHAPTER ELEVEN

VICTORY OVER GUILT

To be a Christian means to forgive
the inexcusable because God has
forgiven the inexcusable in you.
~ C. S. Lewis

A guilt-plagued mind saps creativity. Much creative energy is consumed when guilt and condemnation plague the mind. Those who do great things do not allow their past failures and mistakes to stop them from moving forward. We have all sinned and fallen short at times. We may wish we could go back and change the past, but we cannot. Our minds can easily go to the place of "what ifs?" Although we cannot change the past, we can improve the future. If we live in the past, we cannot proceed forward. The way to be free of previous mistakes is to accept freedom through forgiveness.

Satan likes nothing better than to hold the past over our heads, reminding us daily of former sins. This will keep us in bondage so that our lives will go nowhere. Satan would like to see us lead guilt-ridden lives for the remainder of our time on earth. Why? He knows with guilt hanging over us, we will believe the lie that we are not worthy to accomplish anything.

The enemy will do his best to hold past sins over our heads. If we allow the enemy's guilt to control our minds, it will stop us from fulfilling our purpose in life. A close friend of mine once told me that the enemy will try to take our pasts and hold them over our heads like swords, keeping us in bondage, afraid to move. However, we are to reach up and grab those swords and plunge them into the enemy. Our pasts are our testimonies and make us who we are. God uses everything for good. We can look at our pasts, see the working of God in all of it, and know that we have been changed for the better because of it. It is the word of our testimony that will be used to bring down the enemy in our life and the lives of others.

FORGIVENESS IS THE KEY

By studying the life of Jesus, we can learn all there is to know about forgiveness. He forgave because of His unconditional love. He was a Shepherd to the lost, a Friend to sinners, and Healer to the sick simply because He loved them. He taught, nurtured, and loved all people—even those we might deem unlovable by our standards. No one was unlovable to Him. He came to give, never expecting anything in return. He was tortured for sins He never committed and suffered the most horrible death imaginable. Even then, in pain inconceivable, He forgave those who were putting Him to death. The very ones who were spitting, laughing, and cursing Him were the ones He was forgiving. He forgave us all for all eternity. This is the perfection of love.

You might say, "Well, that was Jesus and He was perfect. He didn't have to endure what we do in this life. How can we be expected to forgive and love as He did?" Jesus went through the same temptations and hardships that we go through in this life and yet He prevailed. We are told in Hebrews 4:15: **"For we do not have a high priest who cannot sympathize with our weaknesses, but One who has been tempted in all things as we are, yet without sin."** He suffered every temptation known to man and still did not sin. He came to earth as a man and had the same feelings that we do, yet He still forgave throughout His life.

FORGIVENESS

As we confess our sins and ask forgiveness, then we are absolutely forgiven. Our sins are gone and washed by the blood of Jesus. After we have been washed clean from sin, then it is erased as though it was never there. And, the wall that has separated us from God is removed. Dwight L. Moody once said, "God has cast our confessed sins into the depths of the sea, and He's even put a 'No Fishing' sign over the spot." Psalm 103:12 states: **"As far as the east is from the west, so far has He removed our transgressions from us."** As we accept the Lord's forgiveness, our minds will be free as well—free to allow His creativity to flow within us.

Along with asking forgiveness from the Lord for our sins, if we have wronged others in the past, we need to ask their forgiveness as well. Guilt will still have a hold on our lives if we have wronged others and not made it right by asking forgiveness. They may or may not forgive you, but that is not your dilemma—it is theirs. Once you have asked forgiveness, you will find new freedom in your life.

There is one more step to forgiveness—we must forgive those who have wronged us. This becomes a little more difficult, especially if wounds have developed from hurts and abuse. As we forgive others, we will be completely free and healed. Otherwise the roots of bitterness, rejection, and so on will still have their hold on us, plaguing our minds. How many times should we forgive someone? Jesus gave us the answer.

Then Peter came and said to Him, "Lord, how often shall my brother sin against me and I forgive him? Up to seven times?"

Jesus said to him, "I do not say to you, up to seven times, but up to seventy times seven" (Matthew 18:21-22).

Jesus knows how hard this life is and He even sympathizes with us. He will also help us as Hebrews 4:16 states. **"Therefore let us draw near with confidence to the throne of grace, so that we may receive mercy and find grace to help in time of need."** I have found by asking the Lord to let me see others through His eyes and feel His compassion, I am able to forgive them. It feels like a cloud has been removed and finally I can see who that person really is. If we ask, He will be faithful to show us why His love is so great for that person. By spending time with the Lord, who is Love, we will become more like Him and take on His characteristics. Receiving His love will enable us to have love for others and forgive them.

Paul tells us in II Corinthians 5:14: **"for the love of Christ controls us..."** If His love controls us, then we would be able to love and forgive as Jesus does. To love, we must die—die to selfish feelings, anger, resentment, bitterness, and discontentment. We must die to those feelings of hurt, turn the other cheek, forgive, and love unconditionally. Solomon tells us in Proverbs 10:12 that: **"Hatred stirs up strife, but love covers all transgressions."** If we love, we can forgive trespasses against us.

When we no longer think about how a person has wronged us, we know we have truly forgiven because the wrongs are no longer consuming our thoughts. If we can learn to live with love as our guide, it will not be so difficult to forgive. To be Christlike, we have to forgive. As we forgive those who mistreat us, the enemy no longer has any power over us in that area. The blood of Jesus breaks that power and we are set free—free to let go of the past and spring forward into the future. The feeling will be much the same as being set free from prison. The confining walls will be knocked down and we will be able to walk forward with true freedom. When the guilt and condemnation of our old issues no longer control us, we can take a quantum leap into freedom, and it is a wonderful feeling.

Every day is a new day, full of new possibilities. When we are forgiven by the Lord, ask forgiveness from those we have wronged, and forgive those who have wronged us, we will be set free—freer than we have ever experienced. Living water will then begin to wash through us, releasing pent-up creativity within us. As we live in this realm of having a clean slate daily, His love will be the guide to fulfilling all that we have been called to do.

We do not know how much time we have on the earth, but as we wake up each day, we have another chance to fulfill that which we have been called to do. Take this new day as a gift from the Lord.

> The greatest thing is to be found at
> one's post as a child of God, living
> each day as though it were our last,
> but planning as though our world
> might last a hundred years.
> ~ C. S. Lewis

CHAPTER TWELVE

YOU WERE BORN TO BE CREATIVE

*What lies behind us and what lies
before us are tiny matters,
compared to what lies within us.*
~ Ralph Waldo Emerson

HOW DO WE BECOME CREATIVE?

As Christians, we have the opportunity to live the most fulfilling, inspiring, and creative lives on earth. You may ask how? Let's look at Genesis 2:7 to answer this. **"Then the LORD God formed man of dust from the ground, and breathed into his nostrils the breath of life; and man became a living being."** Wherever God breathes, He brings life, so breath represents life—man is breathing because of God's breath. As we breathe, the breath of God is flowing through us, which means we have His life and His creativity circulating through us.

II Timothy 3:16 states: **"All Scripture is *inspired* by God and profitable for teaching, for reproof, for correction, for training in righteousness"** (emphasis mine). The Greek translation for **"inspired by God"** is "divinely breathed in," so from this we can see that God breathed on His Words. The Bible contains God's life— His inspired Book. By reading His inspired Word, the flame of creativity will begin to flow within you.

Let's take this a step further in I Thessalonians 1:5:

> **"For our gospel did not come to you in word only, but also in *power* and in the *Holy Spirit* and with *full conviction*; just as you know what kind of men we proved to be among you for your sake"** (emphasis mine).

The Greek word for **"power"** here is *dunamis,* which literally means "force, miraculous power," and is also where the English word "dynamite" was derived. We have this type of dynamite power available to us—the inspiration of God!

We can count on the Holy Spirit to lead and guide us, for He lives within us. We have dynamite power *and* the Holy Spirit available to us. There is no greater help than this.

The Greek text for **"full conviction"** could also mean "certainty" or "full assurance." When we are doing what God has called us to do, we have the full assurance that we are doing the right thing and inspiration will flow through us. Mediocrity should have no place in anything we do because our creativity has the breath of God upon it, giving us the power to do miraculous and creative things!

YOUR PURPOSE WILL BE MADE CLEAR

One significant part in the first *Lord of the Rings* movie is when Frodo is talking to Gandalf in the mines of the dwarfs. Frodo, a Hobbit and the ring bearer, was carrying a heavy weight as he said, "I wish the ring had never come to me. I wish none of this had happened." Gandalf replied, "So do all who live to see such times, but that is not for them to decide. All we have to decide is what to do with the time that is given to us."

Frodo had a difficult destiny to fulfill, but he decided there was no choice—he had to accomplish what he had been called to do. He knew the ring had to be destroyed and he was the one who had to do it. And yes, the ring was destroyed.

Sometimes the Lord will give us something that may seem impossible to accomplish. But we can be assured there will always be a way. If there was not a way, He would not have given us the task. This does not mean it will be easy because in all probability it will not. At times we will be stretched to the limit, but when the task is completed there will be an even greater sense of accomplishment. We must always keep in mind that the task He has given us must be finished—there is no turning back once we begin to walk forward.

Just as Frodo had to constantly fight enemies to fulfill his ultimate destiny, we will as well. We have an enemy who seeks to destroy every work that God has given us to do. We must remember I John 4:4: **You are from God, little children, and have overcome them; because greater is He who is in you than he who is in the world.** God is the strength that lives within us. He will enable us to overcome and do all He has called us to do as we turn to Him.

We have an appointed time to be on the earth. The Lord has known this from the beginning of time. It is up to us as to what we will do with the precious time He has given us. We all want to leave fruit that remains when we are long gone. The late Erma Bombeck once said: "When I stand before God at the end of my life, I would hope that I would not have a single bit of talent left and I could say: 'I used everything you gave me.' Then the Lord would say: **'Well done good and faithful servant'"** (Matthew 25:21 NIV).

This is your chance—there is still time to accomplish something of lasting benefit. You can leave a legacy to leave behind—something that will not perish when you leave this earth. Do not let time slip away, as can so easily happen. Determine not to waste another day.

WHAT DO YOU WANT TO ACCOMPLISH?

Is there something you have always longed to do? Most likely this is what you were born to do. There are certain talents deep within you that will enable you to fulfill your destiny. Maybe you want to write a book or song; perhaps you feel called to be a pastor or teach. You may be called to be a scientist or engineer, ready to discover something that will change the world. You may be talented in singing, administration, counseling, or artistry. The talents and gifts go on and on. But you have something unique that only you can do because God has gifted you with that special talent.

How do you know what your calling is? Once you find out, where do you begin? The following steps are guidelines to help you walk forward and proceed toward fulfilling your destiny.

FULFILLING DESTINY'S CALL

1. The first step is to seek the Lord with all your heart and get to know Him.

The greatest commandment is to **"...love the Lord thy God with all thy heart, and with all thy soul, and with all thy mind, and with all thy strength..."** **(Mark 12:30 KJV).** Before you will be able to walk in your purpose to the fullest extent, you must know the One who called you. Your love for the Lord is what will draw you into a closer relationship with Him, enabling you to fulfill what He has called you to do.

A relationship means "a connection by blood, marriage, or kinship." You entered into a blood relationship with Jesus the day you were saved. You acknowledged that He died for your sins on the cross. As this relationship progresses, you will begin to understand that your communion with Him is through His blood, for it is your lifeline to Him.

In your daily time with the Lord, you will find that your relationship deepens. As you share what is on your heart, you will find that He will respond likewise. He simply wants you to take the initiative to come to Him and then He will come to you. Proverbs 8:17 states: **"I love those who love me; and those who diligently seek me will find me."** There is no question that you will find Him if you seek Him.

Also, during this time with the Lord, He will begin to lay the foundation upon which your purpose in life can grow. Your foundational structure in Him must be strong to firmly hold the weight of what you are to do.

Study His Word daily and allow His Words to permeate deep within you. Remember, it is His living Word that will inspire creativity. This is what will begin to flow through you as you read His Word.

2. As your relationship deepens with the Lord, ask Him to reveal His purpose for your life.

While you are growing in your relationship with the Lord, begin to seek Him concerning your specific purpose. You may already know what you are supposed to do because it is so much a part of you. But as you ask, He will begin to reveal the depth of that purpose which He has designed just for you. You will know when He speaks these things to you because it will be confirmed in your heart, and there will be no doubt that this is indeed what you are supposed to do. This purpose will be His heart's desire, but it will also be what you have always longed to do. If you will spend quality time with the Lord, getting to know Him, you will learn His heart concerning matters in your life.

He chose you to leave lasting fruit behind as John 15:16 states: **"You did not choose Me, but I chose you, and appointed you, that you should go and bear fruit, and that your fruit should remain..."** (NKJV).

Once you have discovered what you are to do, never lose sight of finishing it. Hold it dear to your heart, just like a treasure you have found. One of my favorite lines in the movie, *The Empire Strikes Back,* is when Yoda is training Luke and he says: "Do or do not. There is no try." Determine to finish your purpose in life, always!

This treasure needs to be shared with others when the time is right, but only you can do this. My purpose in life is not yours, and yours is not mine. Yours is truly unique to you, and others need what you have to give.

Do you have the perseverance to finish what you have been called to do? This is for you to decide. But I will say this: You will never be truly satisfied with your life until you accomplish what you were born to do.

God wants His purposes to be accomplished on the earth. So, what happens if you do not accomplish your purpose in life? This may be hard to hear, but someone else who has the heart to complete this purpose will be given the task. Determine now that you will never let go of your purpose until it is accomplished.

3. We must receive training to walk in the fullness of our purpose.

Wellington Boone once said, "God doesn't call the equipped, He equips the called." Once you know your purpose in life, you will become excited and may want to immediately start walking in it. But it is very important to wait until you have been trained and released. It almost always takes training to hone the skills within you. You may have to go to school and obtain a degree. But whatever the training, do it! As you train and work daily toward achieving one goal at a time, you are taking the necessary steps to eventually fulfill your purpose in life.

Dr. Samuel Grimes wrote: "Some people say, 'God will never ask me to do something I can't do.' I have come to the place in my life that, if the assignment I sense God is giving me is something that I know I can handle, I know it is probably not from God. The kind of assignments God gives in the Bible are always God-sized.

They are beyond what people can do, because He wants to demonstrate His nature, His strength, His provision, and His kindness to His people and to a watching world. This is the only way the world will come to know Him."[1]

Most of the time we will feel totally inadequate to do what God has called us to do. That is okay. God will give us what it takes to accomplish His will, but it will take work and perseverance as we have discussed. The question is: Will we accept or give up what you are supposed to do? The choice is ours.

GO FOR THE TRAINING!

It is amazing how God will set up the training that will enable the goal to be achieved. Let me explain what happened in my own life. Before I became the managing editor for MorningStar, I felt I was supposed to write a book. I had never attempted such a project and was at a loss as to how to accomplish such a huge goal. However, God did provide the training that I needed to accomplish this goal.

You might think because I am an editor that I was an English major in college, but I was not. Though I loved English classes and enjoyed writing college papers and reading classics, my degree is actually in Home Economics with a certification in Early Childhood Education. I taught first and second grade for nine years. But then one year my own children were attending a private school that needed a high school English teacher. They could find no one, so I volunteered to take the job. Amazingly, I was able to brush up on all the skills I would need later as an editor. I had no clue that the future held an editing position for me. But God knew.

I felt it was time to move to a small mountain town in North Carolina, and I knew God would provide a job if He wanted me to move there. So, I visited the area and interviewed for a teaching position at a charter school. I was offered the job, signed a contract, and we moved there during the summer. However, after only two months of working at the school, it closed, and I had no job! I had just sold my house and moved to a new area, and now had no job with a family to support. But I still knew God had a purpose for me in the area. I was not ready to give up so soon.

Soon thereafter, my brother, Rick, offered me an editing position with MorningStar Publications. I accepted, but it was difficult to work in a completely new profession. I studied, took some classes, read books on writing, editing, and grammar, and practiced what I learned daily. I took the managing editor's position with MorningStar, and have been in that position for more than five years now.

God not only provided an English teacher's job to review the skills I would need to be an editor, but since I had been working on my first novel entitled, *The Chosen Path,* for almost four years, I was able to finish it. Because I was placed in an editing position, I worked on everyone else's writing, which ultimately enabled me to become a better writer. I began writing articles for *The Morning Star Journal*, which also enabled me to put to practice all that I was learning. It seemed the floodgates were open and I was finally able to finish the novel. In 2003, after eight years of work, *The Chosen Path* was published. I cannot tell you how good it felt to finally hold my book the first time.

God is so wonderful! He knew all along that I would love writing, even though I did not know it because it was buried so deep within me. He orchestrated every circumstance in my life to prepare me to walk in my foremost purpose in life—writing. Now, I am even teaching what the Lord has taught me about writing, as well as other areas of revelation.

I have mentioned how my training came, but training can come in many ways. The Lord is always the best instructor, so instruction and clarity of vision will come from Him. He will begin training you as you draw closer to Him. Also, as you read the Bible, many areas of your purpose that have seemed blurry will begin to be clarified, showing you the way to walk forward in training or whatever needs to be done to accomplish what you were born to do. The Lord may send someone to help guide and train you. Learn from others—many have already cleared the paths before you and can give guidance.

Study books in your field—you will be amazed at the training you will receive. It may have taken others a lifetime of study to write what they have learned, but you can read what they have learned in just a few hours. Glean everything you can and practice those skills. As mentioned, it may take schooling to actually be trained in your area of expertise. Whatever it takes, do it! There will be a way for all the details to be worked out for the training. Stay in prayer and watch the Lord work.

Your training will be going on constantly, and there will always be more to learn and do. Once you receive a glimpse of what you are supposed to do, the vision will continually be increasing as you grow in Him. Who knows what deep treasures are hidden within you? You will discover more as you are faithful to walk in what you do know. The living water will flow as you begin to faithfully walk in what He is showing you to do. The Lord has begun giving individuals many gifts to enable us to blossom in creativity. As these gifts are shared and used, more gifts will be given. They will begin to multiply because **"He who is faithful in a very little thing is faithful also in much... (Luke 16:10).**

When we are walking strongly in our purpose in life, we will then be able to guide and train those with the same calling. The whole body needs to be working, training, and functioning individually and corporately—not just parts of it. We are all different and what we are called to do will be flavored with our own uniqueness. These diversified ministries and callings are needed in the body of Christ so that we can all work together and fulfill the purposes of the Lord. We can learn from each other and what we can glean from one another will help us grow stronger as a body.

Remember, it takes faith and patience to inherit the promises, and most of the time they do not come quickly. As we are faithful in the areas to which the Lord has called us, we will find that He will give us more and more to do in the very areas of our heart's desire.

4. Determine to let nothing stand in the way.

The key to fulfilling your ultimate destiny is to never stop until it is done. This is the tragedy with many. Most have good intentions to begin with, but when they find the cost is too great, they stop.

The Bible states in Hebrews 12:1 that we must be careful to **"... run with patient endurance and steady**

and active persistence the appointed course of the race that is set before us" (AMP). Running at a steady pace will give you the strength to endure the course placed before you. A runner does not immediately run one mile, but steadily builds endurance until he can successfully finish a mile run. While pushing forward, the runner is taking new ground. With training, the runner will soon be running two miles, then three, and so on. As you proceed with training in your calling, you will become stronger. This training is what will ultimately enable you to fulfill your purpose in life.

Do not let anything stop you from accomplishing what you were born to do. Remember, the enemy will try to stop any work that will leave lasting fruit. Resolve to fight and overcome him at every corner. We want everything we do to be fully ripened, in its best state.

NOAH

When I think of someone who was determined in the Bible, Noah comes to mind. During Noah's time, the earth was filled with violence. People had turned away from God, and He was very sorry He had even made them. God came to Noah and told him He was going to send a flood upon the earth to destroy every living thing. He also told him to build an ark so that he and his family would survive. He gave him specific directions on how to build the ark, including details on the size, for it was to hold two of every unclean, living creature and seven of every clean, living creature. Noah did not doubt; he simply started building the ark, believing that God's words were true.

The ark's dimensions were to be 450 feet long, 75 feet wide, with a depth of 45 feet. These dimensions are about the same size as an ocean liner. Can you imagine what the people were saying to Noah and his sons as they were building this ark? Here he was building this huge boat on dry land, with no water near it. He had to totally ignore those around him who were making many derogatory comments, and simply believe God. Every day Noah steadily worked, determining he would finish the ark, and he did. This was not a fast work; it took Noah 120 years to build the ark! Because of his perseverance, the ark was ready when it was time for the flood, and his family was saved.

If you are working toward fulfilling your purpose in life, do not let discouraging words stop you from doing it. When we have something of worth to accomplish, we cannot worry about what other people may think. If God has given us something to do, we must do it at all costs. He is the One we are seeking to please, not those around us. Our focus and determination must be as one.

RUTH

One of my favorite women in the Bible is Ruth. I love her character; she was giving, kind, loving, and determined. As we take a glimpse at the story of Ruth, we will see it was her determination that enabled her to reach her potential in life.

Tragedy had struck Naomi's family. Her husband and two sons had died, leaving her with two daughters-in-law, Orpah and Ruth. Naomi decided that she must return to her homeland of Judah. She told Orpah and

Ruth to go to their own people. Orpah did decide to leave and go back to her own people, the Moabites, but Ruth determined to stay with Naomi. She said to Naomi:

"Do not urge me to leave you or turn back from following you; for where you go, I will go, and where you lodge, I will lodge. Your people shall be my people, and your God, my God.

Where you die, I will die, and there I will be buried. Thus may the LORD do to me, and worse, if anything but death parts you and me."

When she saw that she was *determined* to go with her, she said no more to her (Ruth 1:16-18 emphasis mine).

Because Ruth followed her heart and determined to stay with Naomi, she was able to fulfill her purpose. She was not deterred from what she believed she must do. Both she and Naomi were blessed because of Ruth's faithfulness—Ruth later married Boaz, her kinsman redeemer. So, Ruth and Naomi were taken care of the rest of their lives by Boaz. Ruth was rewarded further for her loyalty by becoming the great grandmother of King David, the very lineage through which Jesus Christ would be born.

When we clearly see our purpose in life, we must determine that we will see it through all the way to the end. Picture determination as a horse in a race with blinders on, not looking to the right or left, but staying focused on the finish line ahead. That, indeed, is how we can finish the course set before us.

We should take heed to the instructions as stated in James 1:2-4: **"Consider it all joy, my brethren, when**

you encounter various trials, knowing that the testing of your faith produces endurance. And let endurance have its perfect result, that you may be perfect and complete, lacking in nothing." We all have trials, but it is the endurance and strength we learn from these trials that gives us what it takes to have victory in our battles against the enemy and to complete our purpose in life. Part of the training comes when we fall; we must not stay down, but rise up and run again, learning to keep the momentum going.

> *I have missed more than 9,000 shots in my career. I have lost almost 300 games. On 26 occasions I have been entrusted to take the game winning shot...and I missed. I have failed over and over and over again in my life. And that's precisely why I succeed.*
>
> *~Michael Jordan*

Why did Michael Jordan succeed? He did not stay down when he made mistakes; he learned from them. He practiced more and perfected his shots until he became one of the best basketball players *ever*. Failure can set us up to win a far greater victory if we will learn from our mistakes.

The Lord will finish the work He has begun within you. But you must first be willing to submit to His training, allowing all that hinders you to be removed so He can clearly show you your path of destiny.

There is still time to do all you have been called to do. That burning inside to produce fruit which remains will not leave until you do it. Yes, there is a sacrifice of time, wants, and desires, but it will all be worth it for eternity's sake.

You have a purpose, an ultimate destiny chosen specifically for you. And if you search your heart, you will discover that dream. Go for it and discipline yourself to work toward finishing it daily. Determine to never stop until it is accomplished. You have been born for **"such a time as this" (Esther 4:14).** We all want to know that we have used all the talents the Lord has given us when we leave this life.

Take courage and embrace your destiny. Today is the day to begin! With proper training and preparation, you will fulfill what you were born to do. The reward will be a relationship of true intimacy with the Lord beyond anything that you have ever dreamed possible. When we at last see the Lord, we want to be able to say: **"I have fought the good fight, I have finished the course, I have kept the faith" (II Timothy 4:7).** And, then He would say, **"Well done, good and faithful servant!" (Matthew 25:21 NIV).** We can hear those words if we continue to press on daily to fulfill our purpose in life as Paul instructed us in Philippians 3:13-14:

> **Brethren, I do not regard myself as having laid hold of it yet; but one thing I do: forgetting what lies behind and reaching forward to what lies ahead,**
>
> **I press on toward the goal for the prize of the upward call of God in Christ Jesus.**

The One that gives us the true power of purpose is Jesus, who is the Light which shines within us. As our relationship deepens with Him, so will our light. Jesus said, **"Therefore, if your whole body is full of light, and no part of it dark, it will be completely lighted,**

as when the light of a lamp shines on you" (Luke 11:36). His Light is the power that will illuminate our pathway to purpose, propelling us forward.

Our calling is before us. May we all embrace the power of His light that He so freely gives so we may accomplish all that we have been born to fulfill. His grace is sufficient for this, and so much more.

> Dream lofty dreams, and as you dream,
> so shall you become.
>
> Your vision is the promise of what
> you shall one day be.
>
> Your ideal is the prophecy of what
> you shall at last unveil.
>
> ~ James Allen, Nineteenth Century English Writer

NOTES

CHAPTER 1

Some information and all quotes for this chapter were taken from *Martha Berry, A Woman of Courageous Spirit and Bold Dreams* by Joyce Blackburn, Peachtree Publishers, 1992. Other information was provided by the Oak Hill Online Museum website: www.berry.edu/oakhill and Berry College website: www.berry.edu

CHAPTER 2

1. Swift, Catherine, *C.S. Lewis,* Bethany House Publishers, Minneapolis, Minnesota, pg. 8. Used by Permission.

2. Ibid, pg. 9.

3. Ibid, pg. 11.

4. © 2000-2004 Pearson Education, publishing as Infoplease. By: Imbornoni, Ann-Marie, www.infoplease.com/spot/narnia-lewis.html. Used by Permission.

5. Ibid

6. Swift, Catherine, *C.S. Lewis,* Bethany House Publishers, Minneapolis, Minnesota, pg. 36. Used by Permission.

7. © 2000-2004 Pearson Education, publishing as Infoplease. By: Imbornoni, Ann-Marie, www.infoplease.com/spot/narnia-lewis.html. Used by Permission.

8. Swift, Catherine, *C.S. Lewis,* Bethany House Publishers, Minneapolis, Minnesota, pg. 92. Used by Permission.

9. Ibid, pgs. 92-93.

10. Ibid, pg. 102.

11. Reagan, Dr. David R., *One Man's Road to Jesus,* Lamb & Lion Ministries, www.lamblion.com. Used by Permission.

12. Ibid

13. Swift, Catherine, *C.S. Lewis,* Bethany House Publishers, Minneapolis, Minnesota, pg. 114. Used by Permission.

14. © 2000-2004 Pearson Education, publishing as Infoplease. By: Imbornoni, Ann-Marie, www.infoplease.com/spot/narnia-lewis.html. Used by Permission.

15. Ibid

16. © Graham, David, Colson, Charles, *We Remember C.S. Lewis,* Broadman & Holman Publishers, Nashville, Tenn., 2001, pg. 28. Used by Permission.

CHAPTER 3

1. © 2002 by PageWise, Inc. Used by Permission.

2. *Label France,* magazine, Ministry of Foreign Affairs, website: http://www.france.diplomatie.fr/label_france/ENGLISH/SCIENCES/CURIE/MARIE.html. Used by Permission.

3. © 2002 by PageWise, Inc. Used by Permission.

4. *Label France,* magazine, Ministry of Foreign Affairs, website: http://www.france.diplomatie.fr/label_france/ENGLISH/SCIENCES/CURIE/MARIE.html. Used by Permission.

5. *NobelPrize.org,* website: http://nobelprize.org/physics/laureates/1903/marie-curie-bio.html. Used by Permission.

6. Hole, Jr. Robert B, Science Hero: Madame Curie, website: http://www.myhero.com/myhero/hero.asp?hero=madameCurie. Used by Permission.

7. Ibid

8. © 2002 by PageWise, Inc. Used by Permission.

9. Nosotro, Rit, *Marie, Curie.* 20 Nov. 2004. website: http://www.hyperhistory.net/apwh/bios/b2currie.htm. Used by Permission.

10. © 2002 by PageWise, Inc. Used by Permission.

CHAPTER 4

1. Wuensch, Christopher, Commentary: Valvano's Message Lives On, *Arizona Daily Wildcat,* Tuesday, December 9, 2003. Used by Permission.

2. Golenbock, Peter, *Personal Fouls,* Carroll & Graf Publishers, Inc., New York, 1989, pg. 28. Used by Permission.

3. Ibid, pg. 28.

4. Jacobs, Barry, *Three Paths to Glory*, McMillan Publishing Co., New York, 1993. Used by Permission.

5. Kindred, Dave, *Washington Post.* Used by Permission.

6. Young, Christopher, The Sporting Eye, March 17, 2003, © The Boston Phoenix, Inc., Used by Permission.

7. Ibid

8. Ibid

9. Towle, Mike, *I Remember Jim Valvano,* Cumberland House Publishing, Nashville, Tenn. Used by Permission.

10. Ibid

11. Dr. Moore, James W. "Never Give Up," http://www.day1.net/ Used by Permission.

CHAPTER 5

1. Beals, Gerald, *Biography of Thomas Alva Edison,* website: http://www.thomasedison.com/biog.htm and thomasedison.com. Used by Permission.

2. Ibid

3. Ibid

4. Ibid

5. Ibid

CHAPTER 6

1. David Michaelis, from his essay, *"The Life and Times of Charles Schulz,"* published in THE COMPLETE PEANUTS, 1950 to 1952, (Vol. 1 Fantagraphics Books, 2004). Quoted with Permission.

2. Gertler, Nat, *Charles Schulz: A Career,* website: http:// AAUGH.com/guide/schulz.htm. Used by Permission.

3. Ibid

4. Berstein, Adam, *Washington Post,* February 14, 2000, *"Peanuts" Creator Charles Schulz Dies,* website: http:// inicia.es/de/edfabra/SchulzObituaryWP.htm. Used by Permission.

5. David Michaelis, from his essay, *"The Life and Times of Charles Schulz,"* published in THE COMPLETE PEANUTS, 1950 to 1952, (Vol. 1 Fantagraphics Books, 2004).

6. Ibid

7. Ibid

8. Berstein, Adam, *Washington Post,* February 14, 2000, *"Peanuts" Creator Charles Schulz Dies:* website: http:// inicia.es/de/edfabra/SchulzObituaryWP.htm. Used by Permission.

9. Hoover, Dennis R., *Peanuts for Christ,* website: http:// www.trincoll.edu/depts/csrpl/RINVol3No2/ charles_schulz.htm

10. Berstein, Adam, *Washington Post,* February 14, 2000, *"Peanuts" Creator Charles Schulz Dies,* website: http:// inicia.es/de/edfabra/SchulzObituaryWP.htm. Used by Permission.

CHAPTER 12

1. Grimes, Dr. Samuel, Determining Your Calling, *The Morning Star Journal, Vol. 14.3.*

Request a *FREE* MorningStar Resource Catalog!

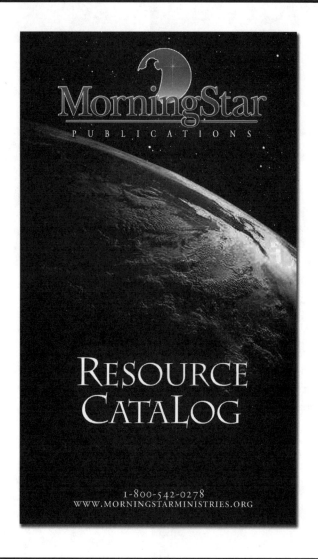